CW01661558

Surviving Bleak House

My Memoirs

LAL KELLY

Copyright © 2020 L.A.L. Kelly

All rights reserved.

The rights of the author have been asserted in accordance with Sections 77 and 78 of the Copyright Designs and Patents Act, 1988.

ISBN: 978-1-8380717-0-7

No part of this book may be reproduced (including photocopying or storing in any medium by electronic means and whether or not transiently or incidentally to some other use of this publication) without the written permission of the copyright holder except in accordance with the provisions of the Copyright, design and patents Act 1988.

TEAM AUTHOR UK
Publishing with you

DEDICATION

I would like to take this moment to thank you for picking this book to read.

This book is dedicated to survivors of abuse everywhere in the world, you are not alone.

And to my family, thanks for seeing me through the dark times, I love you.

INTRODUCTION

I know not all women dream of happy-ever-afters, and knights on horseback to rescue them from the mundane, or for a life of married bliss for eternity. I didn't either. I just wanted to marry a nice average bloke, have two children, buy a house and spend the rest of my life pulling each other up and having fun. I wanted to raise my family, the stereotypical two-point-four nuclear way. I wanted film nights, board games, good food, annual holidays, and most of all, I wanted my children to feel safe and loved. I didn't think that was a far stretch.

Unfortunately, that wasn't to be. You don't always get what you want, I learned that the hard way. It was a long lesson, one that still affects me to this day.

I was just sixteen when I met *that man.* He was eighteen years old. Our encounter occurred when a friend wanted me to join her in hooking up with his friend, wing woman stuff. That man had a car, quite unusual for the time and he could also get booze.

The four of us often went driving around. My friend and her man in the back seat, and me keeping company with the other in the front. It was fine, I didn't mind it. Then one day he turned up outside my house alone, wanting to go for a drive. I said no the first few times, but he persisted until I agreed and slowly, we became a thing.

I can't quite say what I liked about him. I think it was the attention. He really did know how to compliment me and make me feel wanted. If I had to pick a feature, it would be his intense blue eyes, which drew me in. Looking back, there was nothing remotely special about him. But he seemed to adore me, and that was how we came to be. We got engaged after a year with a twenty-pound ring from Argos and married three years later when I became pregnant.

The wedding was basic, a cheap dress from the market, a quick registry office 'I do', a handful of family, and my mum made some butties back at the house. I mean, not quite my dream wedding, but we were married on a budget.

My married life was not the happy experience that I thought it would be. I can't say that we constantly fought because we didn't. But he had no interest in helping with the kids. He was out a lot, and I realised I was raising them by myself. We had a life on benefits as he just didn't seem interested in working. As for me, his stance was clear; wives should be at home raising the kids and keeping house.

I began studying, doing voluntary work and learned to drive. He made all of these very difficult for me until I abandoned everything. He could do what he wanted, but I was very limited. We didn't have holidays or day trips. Our life was pretty bland.

The biggest thing for me was that he had one side for me and another for everyone else. He would generally talk to me like shit but was absolutely lovely in front of other people, which is why it was so hard to get support when we split up. No one was willing to believe he was that bad. The hardest part of breaking up was losing friends. He would tell anyone who would listen that I was making things up because I was a nasty, bitter bitch that wanted to hurt him. I was shocked to find out that people believed him. That was hard, but the worst was yet to come.

I tried to stay in the house, but he made it impossible with his constant harassment and threats. In the end, I had no other option but to move to the Women's Aid refuge far away.

'Although the world is full of suffering, it is also full of the overcoming of it.'

~ Helen Keller

CHAPTER ONE

AUGUST

"Mickaaaaaaay, will you get here now, you little shit."

I stepped out of my brother's car and stared at the red brick building that was to be my new home. A woman stood outside the doorway. Looking at her, I would say she was about thirty-five years old. She had long, brown, curly hair, half-scraped back like it had been styled in a hurry. She wore no make-up and looked a bit pestered with a frown upon her freckled face.

"Hiya. Welcome to the madhouse. I'm Vic. Micky, will you fucking stop it! Sorry, nice to meet you. Let's go before you drive me mad." Vic walked off hastily, pushing a pram, and dragging a boy of around eight years old along at her side.

I continued to stare at this building as my brother took two bin bags out of the boot of the car. The brick walls were not homely. It looked like some sort of clinic or office building. Except there were bars on the windows.

"Here we are then, Lal. Grab the bab, and I'll take these in for you."

I took my nineteen-month-old baby out of the car, and my two young girls, who were aged five and six. They climbed out and followed me to the door. The solid wood door was dark and uninviting. But I was here for a reason and had to press the bell. A voice piped up on the intercom.

"Hello?"

"Erm, hi. It's Lal Kelly. You had a phone call. I was told to come here today."

"All right, come in."

The door buzzed, and my brother walked in with my bags to the sound of a booming and gruff voice.

"No men inside the building, please leave." I was startled. The voice came from behind a glass window, and a surly, old-ish woman sat there with a yellowing perm and heavy glasses. We were in a small corridor which was blocked off to the building by a security door. It was a small space, especially with me, three children, my brother and two bin bags in there.

"OK, Sis. I'll leave you to it. See ya soon. Take care." I hugged him tightly.

"Thanks, G." Once my brother left, the reality of the situation hit me. I had a sinking feeling. This building with its hard floors and bland walls was my new home, my escape from my previous life and the person who had forced me to make the drastic decision to abandon everything and move to this godforsaken place. All I could do to keep myself on track to a better future was to keep telling myself that this was the way out. The light at the end of the tunnel. The solution.

"I'll buzz you in. Leave your bags there," the voice boomed.

I went into a small office. There was nothing exceptional about it. It was practical with file littered desks and a computer and telephone that looked like they had been installed in the nineteen-eighties. The decor had seen better days too, come to think of it. So had this woman, who was scrabbling about for forms and a pen.

"I'll call through for Sandy from the crèche to come and take the children for the rest of the session. We have children's sessions three mornings a week from nine until twelve. It gives you mums a break." Sandy soon came and ushered the kids away. "Right then, let me see. I'm Pam, and you're Lal?" I had told her my name, but I think she needed confirmation. I nodded. "I will give you some time to fill these forms in, basic procedure, personal details and the like. Then I will tell you about our service and explain to you the rules. How does that sound?"

I didn't actually think she wanted an answer. It was more of a directive, so I didn't feel the need to OK it. I just began filling in the details, while Pam sparked up a cigarette. That explained the yellow hair then. I smoked myself, so I didn't mind so much.

"Right then, let's see if that's in order. You will need to get yourself a doctor and a dentist, for you and the children. Then you will need to give me the details."

"Um, OK. Do you know where I should register for these? Do you have names of dentists and doctors?" What she said next did surprise me a little and didn't do well for first impressions.

"You have been told how to do everything for years. You need to learn to do things by yourself now."

I was a little taken aback. I went on to explain to her that I had been living alone for a year, and had to move because of the constant threats and harassment that I had received from my ex-husband and that I was more than capable of doing things myself, thank you very much. To which Pam simply replied, "Oh." Pam informed me that they had yellow pages available when I needed them.

The rules were simple. I had a curfew of ten o'clock, and I couldn't stay out for more than two nights a week. I had to be considerate of other residents, and I had to carry out cleaning chores every day. The chore would be dependent on the room allocated to me. If I didn't clean three times, I would be evicted.

Pam showed me to my room. It was quite large, and it housed two sets of bunk beds, a cot, a single bed, and a sink. It had no carpet or curtains. There were just plastic blinds and visible bars on the window. Pam must have noticed me staring.

"The bars are to keep men out, and not just exes. Women have tried to sneak men in here before. You will meet Linda later. She will give you bedding."

I then followed Pam as she showed me the shared bathroom, with the warning to always wash the bathtub before use, then the lounge and playroom, which were very bare. Next came the kitchen, and, oh dear, another eighties installation.

"There are two kitchens. You are in this one because each room is allocated a kitchen. You have a cupboard with plates and cups. You also have this fridge."

There were a couple of women sat at the table, fags in hand, drinking coffee. They didn't raise an eyebrow. I imagined that they probably saw this a lot. I felt like the new girl at school, except that no one seemed interested in me. Pam continued to show me the garden and laundry room.

"The kids finish in twenty minutes, so I will show you where to get them from. I will give you a grocery pack and leave you to it. I will ask Linda to sort your bedding out when she comes in. Anything else you will learn as you go along."

The first thing I noticed in my grocery pack was a small jar of coffee, which was heaven-sent right now. After dropping off my bags, I went to the kitchen for a brew and a fag. It was now empty, so I spent fifteen minutes contemplating my life. How had my life come to this? Two hours ago I was in my home, close to family and friends. Two days before, I believed that my life would be spent in my house. It wasn't much; it was a council property. But it was in a good area, by a good school, and it had my heart in it. I had decorated it, furnished it, and given it love. Then, out of absolute desperation, I contacted the local Women's Aid, and my life changed almost immediately. I had a meeting with them one day, and by the next, they had a room waiting for me.

They strongly advised me, urged me even, to take this room. It was in the Women's Aid refuge about forty miles away. I would lose everything but would gain my freedom. So, I grabbed the bull by the horns, and I felt like William Wallace.

* * *

The children had been asleep for a good hour when I decided to get ready for bed. I stared at myself in the mirror. I looked a little soul-less. My eyes didn't sparkle anymore, and I was almost a shadow of myself. I had little wisps of long, auburn-brown hair covering some of my face. It was a little frizzy, but I didn't care too much for my appearance. As long as it went into a ponytail, I was happy with it.

In the summer, my freckles come out, and with my olive skin, I looked almost Italian. I had an awful sense of style, this I knew. I didn't wear make-up, it was too much effort, and I would cover myself up with clothes. I hadn't shown flesh above the knee or below the collarbone since I was fifteen as my ex-husband didn't approve. I had an amazing figure then with curves where they should be. He knew this and didn't want me to get any male attention.

Now, however, I was a little overweight. Three kids will do that. I didn't like to look at my body. I hated long mirrors and avoided changing rooms. I just bought oversized jumpers and hid behind my weight. I knew that I was using my weight as a barrier. It kept the attention of men away, and I didn't want to encourage anyone to desire me. I would have liked it to be one less worry, but he found other ways of using my looks to find fault.

I looked in the mirror and, just for a moment, I felt free from all that shit. Then the reality hit, that by now he had probably discovered that I had fled my house and he would be enraged. This made me anxious, a little terrified even. But it was done. Now I just had to wait for the fallout.

As I prepared for bed, I stood over the sink, and as I took out my single diamond earring, it fell down the plughole. I let out a whimper as this was not just any earring, this was given to me by my best friend, Zara. We both had an upper ear piercing, and we were both to wear an earring each. Zara had given me this earring just the day before because she was so upset that I was leaving. She had wanted to give me something special and look what I had done with her gift. Maybe HE was right. Perhaps I didn't deserve nice things.

Zara was utterly lost when I left. Her father was terminally ill with brain cancer, and she needed me. In fact, being there for her sort of made me forget my own problems for a while and knowing that I wouldn't see

Zara for some time, almost felt like I had lost my therapy, my chance to escape for a spell here and there. I felt so guilty leaving her. I didn't tell her where I was going, or anyone else for that matter, because I wanted them to be safe. Her not knowing was for the best. I had my mobile phone, and that was my only link with my previous life, that was my new support network.

The first night was a bit surreal. Not least because the beds were metal-framed, and the mattresses were plastic coated, as were the duvets and the pillows. Even though Linda had supplied bedding, the noise of plastic crinkling with every move was prominent. In addition, the room was hot as it was a summer's night in August, and the windows didn't open. The fan provided did nothing.

The worst thing was the noise from the corridors. People's chattering echoed, and babies were crying. It was almost haunting. Like the sound, one would imagine, coming from a ghostly abandoned orphanage. Unsurprisingly, I didn't sleep. It was a long night, and I questioned my decision to move here. The reason was not that I was sick of the harassment, but because my eldest daughter, Ellie, was.

Ellie had begged and begged for weeks for us to move. She cried constantly, but once she uttered the words, "Mummy, I want us to leave this house so that Daddy can't hurt you anymore," then I knew it was time to leave. The one thing that got me through ten years with him was knowing that I was sheltering the kids from it. Now they were involved, I had to protect them, and Ellie's pleas tugged at my heartstrings so much, I had to stop my girl from hurting.

Breakfast time the next morning kick-started a mix of feelings. It felt like I was invading someone else's kitchen. There were several women and children in there too. I acknowledged them in turn with a nod and a wry smile. I wasn't the most outgoing person and didn't sit comfortably with strangers.

I prepared breakfast with the cereal we had received as part of our grocery pack, so we had food at least. A woman began speaking to me, asking if I had moved in yesterday, and how my first night was. I was glad of the icebreaker and, noticing that she had a child, I asked her advice about local schools. It was the summer holidays so I couldn't do much about getting the children into school for a couple of weeks. But just finding out this information would make me feel like I was doing something constructive.

The local school was literally across the road, and they were aware that they would get temporary students from here throughout the year, and would accept them as they came in. I also found out that they had a box of hand-me-down uniforms in the office, as women here couldn't always pay for them, not least because benefits could take time to sort out. I realised that I would have to accept a change of thinking. My children had never had hand-me-downs, and I didn't see why that should change now. But I was at the mercy of the benefits agency and support workers. Living day-to-day, I had to accept any help I was offered.

The kitchen wasn't so bad. Some women spoke to each other, and some just sauntered in and out like shadows. It seemed that the women with children stayed in the kitchen, but women without seemed to come and go. Another thing I had to accept was smoking in the kitchen around the children while they were eating. I had smoked in front of the children, so I couldn't be critical. It was just that so many people seemed to smoke in here. The ashtrays on the table were full and stank. But as I felt like I was in someone else's home, I had to accept this, and I too joined in.

I sat for a while in the kitchen as the children finished their breakfast, and I had a coffee. I was listening to the chat, nothing meaningful, but it felt a bit like a community. I felt like this wasn't going to be too bad. I thought the sense of understanding from some of these women was due to one common factor - that we were all in here for the same reason. I hoped this would lead to mutual support.

Pam entered the kitchen and told me she was going to make an appointment with the benefits agency and housing department. I was to come to the office when I had finished breakfast, which carried another rule, always wash up immediately and put your things away, including communal utensils.

I went to the office and got the details of my appointments. I asked Pam if she could direct me, but, as with the previous day, she wasn't forthcoming with help. She had made the appointment; it was my job to get there. I think my idea of the duties of a support worker were very different from hers. For her, it seemed that help was to be given sparingly and grudgingly as if it were too much effort. From my perspective, I was a young mum who had just been placed in unfamiliar territory. I was in unusual surroundings in an area I had never been in before. I hadn't had time to work out the lay of the land and yet here I was being given an address and told to find it with no navigational tools. Thanks very much, Pam!

I did manage to get some directions, but I still wasn't confident that I would find the place. I also asked one of the women in the kitchen, who was very forthcoming with some helpful instructions on how to locate the place and how far away it was. She also told me where to find a doctor and a dentist too. First lesson here, if in doubt, ask a fellow resident.

I left early just in case I got lost. I actually relished the idea of going for a little walk around the area. It would ease the kids' boredom and allow me to find my bearings and see what the high street was like.

The town wasn't very far, but to get to it we had to walk through a housing estate which looked like a slum. The houses were the old-style council properties in need of new windows, with metal fences. Not one house seemed to show any pride to it. Plants were neglected, the grass was patchy and paths were strewn with old toys and litter. Old, crappy cars lined the street. It was like something from a welfare documentary. The odd person I saw here and there looked like they had no pride in themselves, and they were a reflection of the houses. I realised that this was 'Roughsville'. This was my new neighbourhood.

The high street seemed OK and had some good shops dotted here and there, and charity shops… lots and lots of them, and a flea market. I didn't realise they still existed.

My appointment with the benefits wasn't too bad. I had been on benefits but had to re-apply because I was in a different borough. The meeting with the housing didn't go as well as I hoped. When I moved into this place, I was assured that the average waiting time for a house was three months, maybe four months maximum. The children and I had decided that we would pretend we were on holiday, in a one-star hotel. But it was OK because we wouldn't be there long and our new life would start in twelve weeks.

The housing, however, painted a different picture. Because we didn't want to live in the local area, the waiting time would be longer. They didn't explain why, it just was. I was a bit disheartened as I didn't like the uncertainty of when I could resettle. I knew I could tolerate all of these big changes because an end was in sight. Now I felt unsure about the future, and I didn't like it. But with no home to go back to, I didn't have any choice.

I noticed a chippy near to the refuge. Perfect! I wanted to ease into the place at my own pace. Once in the kitchen was enough for one day. We ate out of the paper, sat on the small rug that Linda had provided and pretended it was a picnic.

I still had my chores to do. I was allocated the toy room and living room. I had to dust, tidy away the toys, brush and mop. Easy-peasy! I took the kids down and set to. But finding urine and excrement in the toy boxes was not what I was expecting. I hesitated for a spell. I just didn't know how to proceed. I knew with certainty that my children would never be allowed to play with these toys. They could have all sorts of diseases on them. And where were the bloody mothers when kids were crapping in the toy room? Filthy sprogs!

Once the shock wore off, I just got on with it. I found Linda to have her sign the job off as complete, and we went to our room to attempt to survive another night. With no idea when we could leave, that's all we could do now, go from day-to-day … surviving.

The next morning, I took the children to Sandy's crèche. There was a queue waiting for it to open, which gave me a chance to have a look at the mothers and guess how old their children were. There seemed to be a good mix of ages. Vic was there. She made small talk and asked if I would be having a coffee. I didn't really have anything else to do and supposed it would be beneficial for me to make some allies in this place.

Away from her two boys, Vic was a much calmer person. She explained that her son Micky was almost deaf, and had learning difficulties, so life with him was a daily struggle. That explained a lot and the poor woman was at the end of her tether. This time, when the children were at the crèche, was when she could be calm. It was almost as if the lines on her face relaxed a little, and her face looked softer.

I got to know a lot from Vic. She was friendly, a little outspoken, but I felt at ease with her. She told me that women would come and go, sometimes in the night and you would never see them. She also explained that the place wasn't just for women who were escaping domestic abuse, but for women in a multitude of different situations. For a start, I learned that the woman in the room next to me was a prostitute who had just come out of prison and had a serious drug habit. Nice!

One thing that Vic made clear was that most women didn't talk much about their relationships. It was like a shameful secret. If anyone wanted to talk about it, they would do so in their own good time, if ever. Vic informed me that once the kids were in bed, a lot of women came down to the kitchen, and they just sat, and talked, and smoked and drank too, more often than not. I wasn't willing to leave the children alone in a strange environment, especially as I didn't know the backgrounds of the people who lived here. I mean, bloody hell, I had a convict living within feet of my door, so feeling safe wasn't an easy task. I decided that for the time being, I would always stay with my children unless they were at the crèche.

* * *

The days were boring here. We would go for walks, sit in the garden, sit in the room, but time dragged. I would chase up the benefits agency, and ring the housing, just to feel like I was doing something. The best day by far came in the first week when Linda came to my room with a small television that had been donated. There were no aerials, so it was a bit useless, but it was a start, and once I got my benefits through, we went to the flea market and bought a cheap DVD player. Just something simple like finding a kid's DVD for a pound seemed like the best thing in the world. Putting the kids in front of the T.V. for a couple of hours was like a bit of luxury for them. Not me though, as I had no interest in kids' films.

A few weeks in and I still wouldn't leave the children in the evenings. The office had a small selection of books. I wasn't a big reader, but the book I picked up and read absolutely changed my perspective on my entire being. The book was called, 'How a Charming Man Makes a Dangerous Lover', and before I even got to the end of the introduction, I was in tears.

The book described my ex-husband to a tee. It was as if it was written about him. The introduction described the most common attributes of an abusive partner. There were things in there that I didn't even know were abuse, yet he had been doing these things. For example, when we first met, he would say, "Do you have to go out with your mates? I wanted to spend more time with you." Also, "We don't need anyone else, we're fine just us two."

I thought this was affection and felt flattered. But according to the book, this was the first form of manipulation to get me away from my friends. Page after page were examples of how I was being manipulated, controlled and separated from friends and family. I was becoming isolated.

He would have a hissy fit if I was ten minutes late and stropping if he didn't get his own way. He would tell me what to wear and how he expected me to look. I thought his pangs of jealousy were because he cared about me so much. But it was so I wouldn't speak to any men because I knew it would upset him.

The book made me realise that I had been controlled in every way, and I hadn't even realised the half of it.

He was controlling me emotionally, psychologically, sexually, financially and, on occasion, physically. I felt like such a fucking idiot. I wasn't stupid. So how the hell had I let one person have such a strangle-hold on me and every aspect of my life?

I always knew that he was a horrible person who treated me like dirt and disrespected me. But I didn't see the true extent of his manipulation until I read the book and realised what he had been doing. I always told myself that as long as the children were happy and didn't see us rowing and fighting, then all was OK.

I felt so stupid. Ignorance really had been bliss. I cried all night, and for the next few days I stayed away from everybody. I couldn't bear to be seen as a victim by anybody, but I honestly didn't know how I would get through this. For the first time since we got here, the light at the end of the tunnel had gone out.

* * *

I hadn't had much contact with my family and friends since I arrived. That was mainly for their safety, as contact with me could be dangerous for all involved. I was waiting for the dust to settle before I reconnected with my old life. I had plenty of text messages from people, like my parents and Zara, but I remained aloof. A part of me didn't want to be in that world because it was too painful to acknowledge what had happened to me for ten years. The other part of me had to accept that my life was never going to be the same.

I knew I could never return to my hometown now. I felt a lot of guilt, knowing that I had left people I loved in a lion's den. Zara sent a message telling me that HE had waited for her at home and threatened to put a petrol bomb through her letterbox if she didn't tell him where I was. Zara was made of tough stuff. But hell, she didn't deserve to be cleaning up my mess. The reason she wanted me to know was to make sure I stayed away.

My parents also got tailed home from the local supermarket. He spent a lot of time tailing my parents or sitting outside their house. I knew a day trip home was also never going to happen. I heard lots of other stories, on the grapevine, where he harassed people while they were shopping, or shouted things on the street. I felt knots in my stomach constantly because of the trouble he was causing for people I cared about. But there was nothing I could do. None of my friends or family wanted him to win this battle. Everyone wanted me to stay away. I realised that I was very lucky. Something that I noticed with the women in here was that they didn't talk about family; it seemed common for these ladies to have no one.

I read that part of the process of manipulation in these relationships was tailored to isolation. Men would work to separate their women from their social network. Looking back, I knew there were incidents where he was trying to seclude me. He had caused rows and tensions between my family and me on numerous occasions. On one stretch of the relationship, I hadn't spoken to my mother for almost two years because of the barriers he had created between us. Saying that though, I had managed to retain most relationships, and he found it hard to penetrate all of my bonds.

My father was a prime example. I was a daddy's girl, and when he noticeably tried to bridge a gap between us, I told him in no uncertain terms that if there was ever a choice to be made between my father and him, that my dad would win hands down. He interfered much less with my circles after that. It was just a shame that the damage with my mother had already been done. But we eventually made up and regained our bond.

I also noticed other ways that he tried to segregate me. Like he hated me spending time with his family and told me that they didn't like me. I had no reason to disbelieve him. He also told me that what happened in our relationship stayed within our walls. He was always keen to keep any rows a secret. He said it was our business. He had been raised to keep his house in order, and that meant to put a face on to the world that everything was good. I learned, to my cost, that keeping his behaviour a secret meant that when I finally plucked up the courage to leave and cited domestic abuse as the reason, very few people believed me, and I also lost some friends because they felt sorry for him.

* * *

I went to the office for my mail. If anyone had a brown envelope, the staff had to witness it being opened, and note what was inside. Brown envelopes meant giros, and when women had giros, they had to pay their rent.

The room I was in cost more a week than my old council house, which had three large bedrooms. However, this was me now, and 'them's the rules'.

While I was there, I got called to Pam's desk as she had an urgent message for me. "You've got to report to the police station."

The police were looking for me because I had disappeared into thin air, and there was a hunt going on for me. The Women's Aid were not at liberty to tell anyone that I was there, as I was 'in hiding'. I went to the police station almost immediately. I presented myself and told them I was in a refuge because my ex-husband had been abusive toward me, and they were happy with that. I was a bit concerned that the police had to track me. But they explained that there had been a report of a missing family and that they were believed to have been taken to Turkey. I thought at first that he was trying to get me arrested for abduction. But the police went on to explain that had I not presented myself to them, that I was going to appear on Crimewatch.

"Families don't just disappear," they said.

Now I realised what he was doing. He wanted to be told where I was. He wanted the whole nation to have eyes on me. I suppose it's cheaper than a private eye. Bad luck, it didn't work!

CHAPTER TWO

SEPTEMBER

I was bemused that I was supposed to be in Turkey. I knew where that idea had come from. He had told anyone who would listen that I had a Turkish boyfriend. I didn't do boyfriends, but I did have a man in my life at that point.

I had met Tony around two months prior to moving when I was at a hen party in the city centre. The bride had given us all a set of dares to perform, and being competitive, I was up for the challenge. Kiss a bald man and get a man's underwear were just two of these dares. Tony was the man, bald and willing to give up his knock-off Calvin Klein's. Result!

I had no problem approaching him. Armed with vodka in my system, and now seeing men as saps to be used, I was happy to be nice to him to win my challenge. Tony seemed like a nice man, a bloke's bloke, out with the lads and on the pull. He was tall and stocky and stood out amongst the crowd.

Once the night was over, I went back to the bride's limousine, and he went to wherever he came from after we had swapped numbers. Tony texted me a lot, and I was going through a tough time, so I began to lean on him. What began as a dare soon became a sexual relationship. I made it clear to him that I didn't want anything serious, but I got the impression that when a man hears 'I don't want to get serious', what they actually hear is 'I'm challenging you to fall in love with me'. Tony was falling, I was not, but he was handy to have around.

He worked shifts, so it was easy for us to see each other without the kids knowing about him. Tony would come along whenever I snapped my fingers. I had a trick to keep him coming back, this man had a weakness for a thong.

I had never had experience of sexy lingerie when I was married. I wore big knickers, nice and practical. I changed to thongs when a friend challenged me to try them. "Better than sliced bread," she said.

I soon realised how effective that triangle of a thong was, poking out above the top of my jeans and it made Tony like putty in my hands. I would always exit his car with a deliberate bend so it was visible, leaving something to keep him hooked. It was a strange concept to me because I was winging it. I didn't view myself as attractive. I certainly wasn't slim, but Tony seemed to find me irresistible, and I was becoming addicted to that feeling of being desired. That said, I was cold to any idea of having a long-term relationship with any man.

Tony was a rock for me while I was in this place. He would come along when the children were in the crèche and keep my mind off things for a couple of hours. We would drive to a park for a walk or find a secluded lane and have sex. We made it work even with nowhere to go. Sometimes we would just go to a café and have a bacon butty. Any time away from that place was relieving. I never questioned Tony's loyalty or character. To be honest, I didn't care. I was in total control of this fling and nothing he said or did bothered me. Little things like him telling me that he had trained as a butcher, and if he wanted to kill me, he could chop me up and dispose of me so I would never be found. That was alongside a conversation about what goes into sausages, which I found more disturbing oddly. He also always referred to himself in the third person and used the term 'stupid Tony' a lot. But none of this mattered because I was in control and could end this at any time. In the meantime, however, I would enjoy spending time with the one person who had absolutely no connection with my past or my abode.

The time had come to enrol the girls at the local school; it was quite literally across the road. The headteacher was approachable, friendly and very welcoming. I had been given second-hand sweaters and had managed to access some emergency funding for the rest of the uniform.

The most noticeable thing here were the looks from other parents, as if my children and I had a toxic disease. I got the impression that these parents would be telling their kids to avoid the new girls because they lived in the refuge. We became used to people avoiding us. We had massive labels attached to us. I don't know what they said, but I would assume it was something like 'trash' or 'dysfunctional'. It didn't feel good to know that my innocent children were judged so harshly because we had been victims of abuse and forced out of our nice house in our nice street.

Double standards sprung to mind with the playground politics of this school. It was situated at the bottom of the very street that was not very unappealing to the eye. Yes, it was Roughsville. So how anyone could judge us when half of the kids here lived in the Roughsville Straits, was a little hypocritical.

It felt good to have the girls in school. It was a bit of normality for them, even though I knew they were missing their friends terribly. Ellie was one loyal little girl. When she made a friend, she was a friend for life. She had two very close friends that she talked about a lot, and the thought of ever trying to replace them filled her with dread. Ellie tended to fall into friendships rather than searching for them.

Nicole, on the other hand, was friends with everybody. Girls were drawn to her, but she didn't have a best friend. She liked to flit between groups as she loved variety and diversity. I had no concerns with Nicole and her ability to make new friends or worried about her being the new kid. Nicole didn't suffer fools.

I was a little worried about Ellie, though. She was sweet to the point of being too nice, and I feared that this could go against her in the sort of school where she was already considered to be different. I prayed she would not get bullied for having such a kind nature. There was nothing I could do. I had to let them go and hope for the best. It was just me and Luke now. What were we to do with ourselves all day?!

Most days were the same. Up for breakfast, take the girls to school and if I could see Tony, I would. The afternoon would be spent watching an old kids' film, or going for a walk, or sitting in the kitchen. It was just repetitive every day. There was always a little drama occurring with someone. Most of it wasn't noteworthy. In fact, I got used to expecting the unexpected. The other women would be moaning or bitching about something like their money hadn't come through, or something had been stolen, or some residents were getting preferential treatment. This was the norm. I was more of a listener, and I liked to keep my wits about me. I didn't want to be swept up with it all, especially gossip, it wasn't my thing, but it kept people from going insane with the same-ness, I suppose.

Another thing I got used to was watching my next-door neighbour tripping about the place. Alison was, as I had been warned, a drug addict and prostitute. She was in this place because she had been released from prison and social services thought it was a good idea to house her with vulnerable families with young children. I had the misfortune to be in the next room, and she would often walk into my room, see me, and claim she was lost. There was a way she walked in, always hunched over with bony fingers creeping around the door like something out of a Dickens novel. Alison was a bit like a Dickens character, the stereotypical Victorian poor woman with bad posture, long lanky hair and pitted skin. If it weren't for the dirty jeans and oversized peach t-shirts she wore, she could have easily stepped out of the nineteenth century.

The thing with Alison was that she wasn't all bad. I got the impression that she wouldn't hurt a fly. When she came into my room, to undoubtedly rob me blind to feed her addiction, she was almost apologetic to see me. There was a strict rule in here about violence and threatening behaviour. She knew that she couldn't intimidate me for fear of being evicted. But whether she was apologetic because she couldn't rob me, or sorry because she didn't want to rob me, I was never sure. I learned quickly in this place to never leave my room door unlocked. I was also soon to learn that my clothes would be stolen from the laundry and food from the fridge. But that became the norm.

This place was one of the biggest refuges in the country and had sixteen rooms. Some were for single women and some were for large families. There was always a mixture when it came to the size of the family unit.

The single women tended to stay away from the kitchen during breakfast time because it was mad busy. These ladies crept out of their rooms after nine into the kitchen to drink and smoke all day. They weren't too concerned about the babies and toddlers being around, and some of these ladies seemed to love babies.

One young woman, Gina, who was around twenty-four, took a real shine to Luke. They had a game they would play where Luke would creep around the door and Gina would pretend to point a gun. She would shout bang-bang and Luke would fall to the ground as if he had been shot. I don't know how this game came to be as I never gave the children guns. They were banned from playing with guns here, but still, this was a thing they did, and I had no problem with it.

I liked Gina, but she was a bit of an enigma. She really kept her story to herself and wasn't that talkative. It was literally 'how's the weather' conversation with her, but I liked her and wanted her to have a good life. Intuition told me she deserved good things to come her way.

There were also women in here that were just always going to have shitty lives. They could be spotted a mile off. Talk about documentary fodder. Some women were just walking statistics. As much as I wanted everyone to have a positive outcome from this hell hole, there were just women who couldn't be helped.

Janet was the type of woman that exuded 'victim'. She was whiney, needy and did not take care of herself at all. I couldn't really age her because her skin was so bad. At a best guess, I would say about thirty.

Janet had two girls under five and a fifteen-year-old son. The girls were so pretty, and they looked different, one being brunette and the other being blonde with beautiful curly hair. They both had startling blue eyes, porcelain skin and cherry lips. This woman must have mated with Adonis and all his genes were triumphant, because Janet was rough. It was clear that Janet had had drug issues, but I wasn't going to judge. As long as people were nice to me, I was nice to them, and Janet and I got along really well. Her son was a bit uncontrollable, but as long as he didn't bother me, I didn't care, not my problem.

I was getting used to which women would be around at different times. Vic and Janet spent a lot of time in the kitchen, and we were getting to know each other well enough. I still spent my evenings in my room with the kids. I didn't want the girls to sit around the kitchen with people smoking, drinking and swearing constantly. There were times when things seemed to chug along smoothly, and other times when tempers frayed. Sunday night was always the boiling point of the week. The reason behind this was the laundry.

All the mums wanted to wash the uniforms on Sunday night. The laundry was a pokey hole with two washing machines and two tumble dryers, and it was first-come-first-served, or it would be if people were respectful of that rule. I soon learned not to give a shit about people waiting for a machine. I would put my stuff next in line to then have people nip in and take my spot. I would put clothes in the tumble dryer only to have people take mine out and put theirs in. It infuriated me.

I stormed in the kitchen one night to find out who was robbing my washing time, to be told, "You should say if you want to use the machines." That little pearl of wisdom came from Janet, and I snarled at her and told her that I had.

It was the first time that I had felt anger since I had arrived nearly a month before. I wasn't an angry person; it was a wasted emotion and solved nothing. But, God help me, I could have had a rock star tantrum in that kitchen and trashed something and possibly someone, especially the person who took my clothes out of the tumble dryer. I actually was scared for myself that such a tiny thing as not getting my clothes dry could possibly end up with me losing the roof over my head. Luckily, I calmed quickly and learned in the future to do my washing on Friday night or Saturday morning.

We began to fall into a routine. All we could do was wait for news of a house, and just eat and sleep, every day. The time here was hard but never a day went by without something going on, and I noticed that there always seemed to be one person that the other women would turn on. This month it was Meera, whose very existence seemed to wind everyone up.

This treatment by the pack animals wasn't her fault. They felt that Meera was getting special treatment because she was Indian. There were certain parts of Meera's culture and religion that meant she did have to do things in a certain way. I was a live and let live type, and I felt for her, especially as children would steal her shoes from outside her room door, which she couldn't take in. They would play knock and run, and I felt it was a little unfair, as Meera really did keep herself to herself, and didn't cause bother for anyone. But the other women wouldn't speak to her. In the kitchen, they would say that she was demanding this and that and if she didn't have her demands met then she would play the race card. I personally never saw evidence of this and felt like I couldn't say anything in Meera's defence in case the pack turned on me and I became next month's dupe. In this place, it was smart not to do anything to stand out. It was a dog eat dog place, and I had my kids to protect.

The girls and I had got to the point where we were used to the noise at night and could all sleep. I had Luke in my bed every night, and hearing his breath soothed me off to sleep. I hated the metal cot that he had, and I struggled to leave him in it.

Our calm nights were soon to become unsettled again. At 5am, the loudest fire alarm I had ever heard, with flashing lights, was activated. The kids were screaming, and we were in a daze with loud banging on the door from one of the night staff telling us to get out! I didn't know what to think. We headed outside and had to stay out for a considerable amount of time. The children were so scared. One of the bathrooms was on fire, and the person who had started the fire was Micky, Vic's eight-year-old son.

It was bad enough that we had to fear danger from the outside, but we now had this threat on the inside. Vic seemed to be split between feeling a little ashamed and apologetic, to passing the responsibility and blaming Micky's disabilities, in a sort of 'shrugging it off' sort of way. All I knew was that I felt like I was never going to sleep again, and indeed I was right, we all struggled for a spell. I felt a little over dramatic, but I genuinely had a niggle that my family were going to be burned alive as we slept. The littlest things in this place always seemed like big things, and I didn't know if that was stress, or because it seemed normal for drama to be exaggerated because so many people did it daily, and I was copying the trend.

My month was going downhill fast. Apart from the lack of sleep, the absolute boredom, being on tenterhooks constantly, and cleaning shit out of the playroom daily, I started to feel a sense of loneliness. Messages from friends and family were winding down like I'd been forgotten about, and everyone was getting on with their own lives.

Tony would call at night when the kids were asleep, and I'd step out of the room and sit on the stone-cold floor in the corridor. He would cheer me up after a long day, and a little bit of me craved his cuddles. He was so good at embracing me wholly, and I felt safe in his arms. Never in the whole time that I had known Tony had he said anything nasty about me. He was too even-tempered, and that's why I was so shocked this night, three months since we met.

I knew Tony liked football, but he was never fanatical about it. But his team had been playing that day and they had lost. He was telling me about it, and I quipped, "Aaaaw, your team are losers?" Tony seemed to lose his usual sense of humour and spat back.

"You're the loser! You live in a fucking refuge, you twat!" I hung up.

Gobsmacked was not the word. What the hell had gotten into him? Seriously? I didn't really seem to feel anything at that exact moment. I went down to the kitchen to make a coffee, and I put my phone on the side.

While I was rinsing my cup, the phone rang, Janet answered, and I was fuming with her, again. She jokingly put on a seductive voice to say hello, then her face fell, and she held out the phone.

"It's for you."

"No shit! Really? Someone on my phone wants me, hmm!" I barked at her. "Don't ever answer my phone again." And when I say 'barked', I mean angry growls from my throat; she had really pissed me off.

That said, Tony was at the end of the phone, and I was now obliged to answer. I answered him short and sweet.

"It's finished, prick, don't call again!"

So that was that. I wasn't emotive, I mean, it felt strange, and I had just lost my only form of escapism from the reality of this place, but I wasn't being spoken to like that. How dare he? It's not like I had any real feelings for him anyway. But I did sort of think, what am I going to do for sex now? Who will I have bacon butties with? Who will desire me? Strangely, I slept better that night than I had for most of my stay here.

The morning after Tony-gate I felt like I had a hangover. It was odd. I had a fuzzy head and was really tired. I struggled to get up that morning, and I put it down to sleeping too well. I thought that's what it must have been. When Luke went to the crèche, I went back to bed.

The whole day was a bit of a haze, and I didn't know what was wrong with me. I was quite healthy but wasn't immune from the odd cold, so thought I must be coming down with something. I slept well the next night, and the night after too, only one thing was different about me, I had disappeared.

I started to feel strange, like I wasn't in myself, as if my consciousness was sort of sitting outside of myself. I felt like I was watching my life rather than living it. Over the course of a few days, I became almost robotic. I did everything I was doing before but in a systematic way. I stopped living and started surviving instead. I didn't know what was happening to me. I convinced myself it was a temporary thing, and I put it down to being stressed for a long stretch, and this was a coping mechanism. I wasn't lying to myself; it was clearly some sort of shut down due to stress, but the scary part was that I wasn't able to snap out of it.

There were a few differences in the way that I was previously, to the way that I was now. Not least because the days seemed to get shorter. I didn't know how that happened. I could only assume it was because I had started to daydream, about nothing, it was just empty, fuzzy space, but I was lost in there, and time seemed to disappear.

I was more than capable with the kids. I got them ready for school, put Luke in the crèche, or in front of the T.V. with a film, and then just waited to pick the girls up. Then another film, then tea, then another film, then bed. Once they were asleep, I was asleep. It was as simple as that. I just wanted to curl up in a ball and sleep until all of this crap was over. It was easier to sleep than to deal with my life.

Even though I never viewed Tony as a permanent fixture in my life, he was, in fact, keeping me sane. He was the only support I had here, and with him gone, I had to face the fact that I had now had nobody. I also had no life, no home, no money and no hope. This was it for me. What the hell had happened to my life? At least before I had my sharp mind, but I'd lost that too, and I just couldn't see how my life was ever going to get any better.

I had this guilt now to add to my mental torment, and I felt guilty because I had dragged my poor children into my downfall. Not only did they have to live here, but they had to live with a mother that was seriously losing the plot. The only thing that kept my mind from slipping into oblivion completely was knowing that I had to fight against this oppressive blackness that was looming. I had to fight to keep my children safe. I had to ensure that no one knew what was going through my mind. If anyone suspected that I was going mad, they might take my children away from me. I had to protect them from a life of 'the system'. No one was taking my children, and I had to snap out of this. I had no intention of continuing to feel like an alien in my own body, living a life through a veil of thick glass where everything was murky. No, that wasn't me. I was too optimistic for this to happen to me. If I was positive, my children were positive, and I didn't want their lives to be damaged. The only thing I could do at this point was fake it, but I honestly didn't know how long I could keep it up for.

* * *

Despite the feeling of not wanting to be found out, and trying to avoid people, I realised that I needed people around me, even if it was just to hear people whinging. In a way, I felt better listening to other people dramas, and I thought what have I got to whinge about? I never felt as if I had a right to moan. I never felt like a victim. It wasn't in my nature to just roll over and give up.

Every so often, a story would come out. A woman would just take the bull by the horns over a coffee and blurt out her entire history like we were a support group. I felt privileged to be a part of it but would usually have mixed feelings. The brainwashed part of me would think I hadn't even been abused. All my ex-husband did was shove me around a bit and spit on me. I could even envisage him saying that to me as I thought it. Then there would be a pang of what am I moaning about? I never had it this bad. This woman has been treated so badly. Then occasionally, I found it hard to believe that all of this happened to me. What the hell did I do to deserve this? What a fucking mug I am. I couldn't believe I let him treat me that way. So other women's tales had a range of effects on me, but they always made me sit up and listen.

One woman who came in with two girls had a story that made me shudder. Her name was Lizzie. I figured she was a little older than me judging by the way she was dressed and carried herself, and I felt that she was similar to me. There were a few of us having a coffee while the crèche was on, and we were having a chat about what would set off our men. Lizzie said that her man was lovely. Yes, indeed, she said he would treat her like a princess. He was supportive, never controlling, and they had a good life. Her ex had a flaw, just now and again, he would lose it. He would go into a proper rage and beat Lizzie black and blue. After he had done this, he would try and make it up to her, and he would be the sweetest, most amazing man, until the next time.

The thing that really got to me was Lizzie confessed that if she knew he was a bit stressed, she would then deliberately wind him up, to get him to beat her. She did this for several reasons. For example, to get it over with quicker, to have her beating at a time to suit her, to make sure the kids weren't around, to name a few.

I told Lizzie that I had never been punched in the face, apart from a few physical altercations; the one time he pushed me down the stairs, and the times he would pin me to the wall and punch the wall beside my head. He also loved to spit in my face, but, my ex had mainly controlled my life with emotional and psychological abuse. How Lizzie responded to that truly stuck with me.

"You know, I would rather take a beating than be psychologically messed with. That sort of abuse is just constant. I wouldn't be able to cope with it," she said.

Lizzie pretty much hit the nail on the head when she acknowledged that headfuck abuse left scars for life that would never heal.

"Physical scars heal, mental ones don't. Give me a beating any day," she finished.

I didn't know whether to feel humbled or to feel like a proper victim. But what I did feel for the first time since my break-up, was that I was legitimate in my accusations, that I had been abused, even though he hadn't physically punched me. I was still the victim of domestic abuse, and I didn't know whether finally accepting that was liberating or not. Only time would tell.

CHAPTER THREE

OCTOBER

I had been here now for just over six weeks, six very long weeks. Time was warped here. For excitement, I would take a trip to the charity shops, or check out my housing application. This was high octane stuff, riveting. The most exciting thing was seeing who would move in that day. Would they have children? Would they be in and out before we saw them? The chances of them being psychotic was pretty high. Sometimes though, women were just highly strung. Sometimes, they were like Sadia.

This woman was like a breath of fresh air. She made it clear that she was there against her will, and she was honest about why she was there. Sadia was on a witness protection programme. She had seen a murder and had to be here. I really felt for her. Something completely out of her control had occurred, and her whole world was turned upside down. There was a genuine risk to her life. On the upside, Sadia was safer here. On the downside, we were all in danger just from her being here. And on the double downside she didn't really relate to us 'battered wives' and could not get how women could let themselves be abused, but that was by the by.

Sadia was mixed race, half Irish and half Arabian. She had dark brown eyes and dark curly hair. She looked Middle Eastern but had the most high-pitched scouse accent. She also had five children, though not all of them lived with her, just her two boys aged eight and seven. The other children temporarily lived with their grandmother.

The two boys looked just like their mum. But funnily enough, her other children looked completely different to each other. Apart from the boys, all the children had different fathers of different nationalities. One had a Chinese father, another had a Russian father, and one had a white British father. Sadia referred to her children as Heinz 57. I thought it was funny. She always quipped about them being different varieties. She was their mum, so it was her prerogative. I liked Sadia being there. She was so straight and to the point. Not everyone agreed with her all of the time, but at least you knew where you stood with her.

October saw a lot of new residents, but this month saw the arrival of the worst type, the ones playing the system. They would lie about being abused to get to the top of the housing register. Using the refuge this way became the norm, and being a resident meant that I saw what the key workers didn't.

It wasn't always apparent at first. The woe-me attitudes were convincing. They really could carry a story. One of the least obvious was my new neighbour across the hall. The drug addict had moved upstairs, and that room was free for Lisa to move in, and we hit it off straight away.

Lisa was around my age, mid-twenties, and had two girls of similar age to my two. The biggest difference between us was that Lisa was a princess. She was so trussed up with hair extensions, fake nails, false eyelashes and designer clothes. Her mini princesses were also wearing the best clothes, and their hair was perfect. The preening that went on daily was unbelievable. I could never afford to take care of myself like that, and I wouldn't want to, it was too much effort. Lisa was able to afford all of the fake beauty and designer clothes because she was a lap dancer. She told me she could earn up to £500 a night. This did make me wonder. What the hell was she doing here if she was earning that type of money?

Of course, the support staff didn't know about her work or her boyfriend that would look after the children while she worked, which was only on the weekends at the moment because of the curfew. But if you wanted a new council house in a new area for you and your boyfriend, then that was the way it had to be.

As much as I hit it off with Lisa, I didn't see her as much as I would have liked as she was out most days. But when she was about, she would style my hair and give me beauty tips. I had never been that girly. I just wasn't raised that way, but it did feel nice to try new hairstyles. Lisa and I were totally girly together; it was different.

* * *

Most days were the same here, but some days would catch you off guard. I received a letter from my solicitor, saying my husband had signed the divorce papers. It was all going to be over in three weeks, and he was getting married the day after our divorce came through. I was elated, I really was, and it was time to partaaaay.

Yet, I became emotional. I was down, and I couldn't understand it. I was divorcing him on the grounds of unreasonable behaviour. He had always maintained that I was a lying drama queen and that I would not ruin his good name. He was always one step ahead of me by whispering in people's ears and telling them I was delusional so that people in the street would stare at me.

He had told the children's headmistress something. I never found out what, but the school had called me in to tell me that they take divorces very seriously and that when things are said they have to put them on the record and protect the children. I was spoken to in a very condescending and frightening way, and I never found out what had been said. It didn't matter in the end as I moved the children out of the school soon after. But this was his way of making me paranoid, and it worked.

He gained extra sympathy votes by moving out on his birthday. That was not the day I asked him to leave, but he just held on until that day so he could tell everyone what a bitch I was for kicking him out on his birthday. Everything was calculated, including his relationship with his fiancée. This whole marriage was to get at me. The girlfriend was there in the first place to make me jealous. He didn't believe me when I said she was welcome to him, so he would constantly flaunt her in my face. This was a cracker though, the wedding. It was hilarious! But for days I was in a strange mood. I couldn't pinpoint a particular emotion. I wanted the divorce, but my mental processing was doing some shit that I couldn't decipher. So, I had no choice but to ride it out.

For days I felt like I could scream at someone. I had to keep it together. I was becoming a master of controlling my external emotions; it was an art. Everyone I met here thought I was the most laid back, horizontal person to grace this concrete box, but inside

I was screaming. I think they were shocked when I finally let out a sign that all was not OK in my world.

Every now and again, we would have someone come in to give us a talk or a class on something that may benefit us for life in the outside world. One day we had to fill out questionnaires on self-esteem and write little sentences on what we should be grateful for. I would usually excel at these things. I was pretty studious, and hell, it was something to break the boredom.

Not today. Today I decided that my time would be better spent making paper aeroplanes and encouraging everyone to sabotage their papers. This did not go down well with the meek lady holding the session. I think she just expected us to all play nicely. Seriously love, don't come into a room of broken women without your backbone. I honestly could not help myself. It was as if a mini demon had taken me over. I just wanted mischief, but I bordered between arsehole and sweetheart, so she just didn't know what to do with me. Not that it would have mattered as no one would have been controlling me that day! Yes, she was upset, and yes, I did end up in the office getting a very stern warning. However, based on my behaviour thus far, and the realisation that the letter I received a few days prior had caused me some distress, they left it at that. We didn't see the meek little taskmaster again. Shame that. Her heart was in the right place.

* * *

October was the month that saw a new resident that would feature high in my life, for both drama and friendship, and even freedom, in a sense. Mary was a heavily pregnant mum of two from a very, very rough area in Liverpool. Jesus! No wonder she wanted to move. The place has one of those reputations that preceded it.

I really liked Mary. She also frustrated me all of the time. Mary was a mousy woman with a laid-back attitude, but she also was a tough cookie. If you were right with her, she was right with you. This woman was tiny, around five feet and she was super skinny, so her bump seemed huge. I honestly don't know how she walked. She had long ratty hair, blonde freckles and the whiniest voice, but I soon got used to it. As much as I liked Mary, she was a tramp, and her kids were unkempt and dirty. They all dressed in trackies. Eeeek!

Lisa was also a scouser, but these two were polar opposites. Lisa was the glamourous scouser with her hair in rollers while curling her fake lashes. While Mary was the rough-as-fuck scouser with her trackies and whingy kids. I didn't feel that I judged her by her appearance. Yes, I was stereotyping her massively, but I liked her regardless. In all fairness, she was heavily pregnant and couldn't be arsed with her appearance or looking after her children properly.

This was the month that the food began to go missing. Mary repeatedly told the children to help themselves, and they did. They were always hungry. One evening, I had made my family dinner. The youngest girl, aged just four, stared at me eating, like a dog watching steak. I couldn't eat my food, and I ended up pushing the plate over to her and telling her to eat it. Yes, it annoyed me that the children stole food, but I was happy that they were getting something. They were so thin and scrawny.

Mary came to rule the kitchen roost, and she had her perch that she sat on every day. It was in the same chair, all day long, and she had everyone running around after her. People made her drinks, watched her kids, took them to school, and even changed the radio if she asked. It was strange that she had this way of directing people, and no one ever seemed to mind.

It was around this time, two months into my stint, that I began leaving the kids in bed in the evening and coming along the corridor to smoke and drink with everyone else. Although we had two kitchens, we would generally gather in one, my kitchen. We had big tables in the middle that would seat eight, and there would usually be around six of us drinking in there. I could hear my children from this kitchen. As for the other kids, usually, someone upstairs would come and say if a child was unsettled.

I began drinking most nights, everyone did. It only cost a few quid for a knock-off bottle of vermouth at the Kwik Save. I wouldn't get drunk off it, just relaxed. That way, I could drink most nights and not be considered an alky. The staff, of course, always popped in to make sure we weren't being rowdy. Sometimes they would sit with us, possibly trying to relate, but it was too much of them and us. They had power over us, and I never went to them for help because I didn't want them to find me out. I was hiding this dark void, and they could never discover my secret. I think they hung about in the kitchen to assess us. But they never felt the need to worry about me or call me in the office. I remained beige.

The kitchen could be interesting, dramatic, full of gossip, or downright disturbing. I saw some disgusting things. I saw people hit their kids and call them names. I heard people talking about drugs. I saw people on drugs. There were overheard phone calls, tears, tantrums and bickering.

My old neighbour had mainly kept herself to herself, and I rarely saw her since she moved upstairs as it wasn't an area that I ventured to. This one morning, I brought the kids to the kitchen for breakfast, and there she was, standing against the table, mumbling incoherently. She was off her face, trying to pick things up off the table that weren't there as she stumbled and ranted. She was a mess. Jesus, it was the kid's breakfast time. Everyone who had entered before me had already gone to the other kitchen, and I ended up doing the same. By then she had already stumbled across the room, flying arse over tit, sprawled over the floor. Then the staff turned up like ants out of a trod-on-crack in the pavement. I never saw her again, thank God.

Evenings weren't always better either. Several evenings were spent with mums picking head lice from there children's hair and disposing of them in one of two ways. They would drop them in a bowl of water to float around, or they would squash them on the table with their fingernails. It was vile. We had to eat at those tables for Christ's sake! Head lice were a massive problem, especially with a lot of girls being there, and the school being rife. It also didn't help that Mary would never do her girl's hair who had visible lice and eggs. I was actually a little scared to prepare food when she was in the kitchen, just in case she shook her hair and a nit flew into my food. This really was one of the things that frustrated me about Mary.

Also, the trouble with head lice is that there will be that one mother who will swear blind that their kids never ever get head lice. Bollocks! Of course, that was Janet. Vic felt that she had to put her in her place on that one, head lice don't discriminate, so get real. I used conditioner and a comb on my girl's hair in the shower, not at the food table. I clearly wasn't the only person that had an issue with some mum's methods, as the staff banned this awful practise around a week after it had begun.

* * *

There was a good group of women residing here now. I mean, they had their flaws, as did I. But we were almost all in the same boat, and this group of women seemed to be here for the long haul like me as it could take three to four months to get a house.

A few women had left. Meera had gone back to her husband. With the constant discrimination against her, I think she decided that her husband was the better option. Sometimes that just happened. Women went back to partners either because they preferred the familiarity, even if it was toxic, or because they couldn't adjust.

It really did take a lot of strength to get through this place. I stopped calling myself a resident and started calling myself an inmate. We would constantly bitch about the bland décor, cold hard floors, plastic beds, bars on the windows, and the staff, of course, would come under fire frequently. Mary began referring to the place as the bleak house, and it stuck. From then on, we would always refer to it as that. Whenever a new resident would come along, we would welcome them to the bleak house. If we were going out, we'd state what time we were returning to the bleak house, and if we were lucky enough to get a couple of days away, we were escaping the bleak house.

It was getting to that time when the days were getting much shorter, so this added to the bleakness of the bleak house. I think I sort of started living in my own virtual novel. If I thought about it, this place was like a drama serial. Corrie had nothing on this place. The drama was daily, and we became so used to it that most things were just passed over as the norm. But not all things. I was about to be involved in my first serious drama, and it involved Sadia.

To be honest, I didn't often let the girls play with the other children, because many of them were just plain naughty. Their mums swore at them a lot, and they had terrible habits like stealing, swearing and fighting. So, it was a rare day to have my girls playing outside, but they were with Sadia's boys, and they hadn't come from an abusive home, so I didn't have anything to worry about.

A seesaw had been donated, and I knew it would last long as the kids literally trashed or stole any toys that came in. But in the meantime, the girls were enjoying playing on it. That was until Sadia's eight-year-old boy decided he wanted to play on it and threw Ellie off. But it didn't end there, she protested and was pushed to the ground and kicked repeatedly. Ellie had never been involved in a violent disruption, and she was inconsolable.

Sadia had been hovering around the building doing laundry and the like and was not aware of what happened. I took my kids to our room and vowed they would never play with those kids again. Sadia was a straight woman, and I knew that she would sort this situation out. She was a fair woman, after all, or so I thought.

Around twenty minutes after the event, Sadia came along. She had talked to her son, and according to him, it was Ellie's fault that she got beaten up because he wanted to play on the see-saw. What the actual fuck?! I really thought that Sadia was a strong independent woman, but I forgot that Arabian men are considered gods and women are merely there to serve them. Obviously, the boy didn't consider Ellie to have any right to that seesaw. Silly Ellie! I didn't exactly go ballistic, but I did tell her she was out of order, her kids were fucking bullies, and she had better keep them away from my children. After slamming the door in her face, I didn't consider any ramifications. After all, my girl had been attacked, so I made the staff aware and left it at that. Children were not punished in this place for any behaviour whatsoever, so it had to end there.

The day passed and evening came, and I was trying my best to stay away from Sadia as I didn't want any more drama. I had a friend who would always send me jokes, it was like we had a 'joke of the day', and I would tell everyone if was good, if not, I didn't bother. This particular evening, my phone pinged, and it was the joke.

"Come on, then. Let's hear it," said Mary.

I told her it was crap because I didn't get it, but the ladies insisted I should tell them. I read out the joke. "A white woman gave birth to a coloured baby. Her white husband wasn't surprised as his wife overcooked everything." It gleaned a few giggles but was soon forgotten, and I didn't think anything else of it.

The following morning, I was called into the office and found myself in a special meeting. Sadia had made a complaint about my racist behaviour and felt uncomfortable living with such a bigot. I was actually in shock, to be accused of being racist was a major blow. I was not racist! They explained that the joke had caused offence. It was then explained to me that racism was not tolerated on any level and that I was going to be evicted.

I was heartbroken for so many reasons, not least because I'd been called racist, but also because I was registered as homeless. Eviction meant the streets as there was literally no accommodation lower than this. Eviction meant the children going into foster homes and me going to cardboard city. That is how serious this situation was. I was in tears trying to explain that I had not seen it a race joke but as a man versus wife joke. After it was explained to me, I then realised I was a bit ignorant about the nature of the joke, but I hadn't meant to be racist.

I was sent away while they had a meeting, and a couple of hours later, I was called back to the office. Sandy had pleaded my case, as she had been my main key worker the entire time, and she believed that I was not racist and didn't mean to offend anyone. She really did fight my corner, and they agreed to let me stay with a warning. Being called racist did upset me, and it stayed with me for the rest of my time there. The whole situation had also made me realise that I could lose my kids and be homeless in a heartbeat. All it would take for this to happen was a woman with a grudge.

A few days after this incident, Sadia herself was called into the office. A complaint had been made about her being racist. I don't know who had made the complaint, and I don't know if someone had done it for me, I will never know. Apparently, someone had been offended by Sadia calling her kids Heinz 57. I wasn't a vengeful person, so I didn't care about whether Sadia had felt that stinging accusation of being called racist, but I actually thought it was a silly complaint. I couldn't understand how someone could be racist against their own children. Sadia was confused, and I agreed with her. They were her kids, so surely it couldn't be racist. But the staff took it seriously, and Sadia too got a warning.

I didn't speak to Sadia that much. She was around, but I pretended she wasn't. The group was getting smaller though, and Vic was leaving. It was such an amazing feeling when someone got a house. All of their excitement rubbed off on everyone, and it would make me think of the day when I would get that letter. Someone getting a house was like a little win for everyone. The best part was that I could go and help Vic with the decorating and cleaning, and I could escape the bleak house for a few hours at a time. Great stuff!

Lizzie was also leaving, but we weren't close enough for me wanting to help her. Sometimes women just wanted to leave and never have any association with this place or the inmates left behind, and that was fine too. It was a good week for Lizzie, though.

One day, I received a message from my sister. She wanted to know how much longer she had to store my 'shit' for. I had come here with just a couple of bin bags of clothes and anything that was super expensive I had left with a few friends and relatives. There wasn't much stuff. Only enough to fill her closet on the top of the stairs, but she decided it was getting in the way. I decided to give it away, and Lizzie had first refusal.

An almost brand-new Dyson vacuum cleaner was the top prize as it was cutting edge at the time, was the most expensive vacuum cleaner I had owned, and it cost hundreds of pounds. There were some other bits and pieces too, but that was a big regret of mine, I hadn't even considered storing it in my room. I wasn't thinking straight, and as I knew my sister wanted my stuff out, I had no option but to get rid of it all. As Lizzie was leaving it just felt right for her to have it.

Giving away such an expensive item did get me thinking about how I was ever going to get stuff when I moved. So, losing the Dyson helped me to think about my future away from the bleak house. I worked out how much money I was receiving, budgeted for food, baccy and wine, and worked out that I could buy new things for the house every week, and that's what I did. I collected new things, and then I didn't feel so bad about losing my vacuum cleaner. Well, I knew I couldn't afford one of those, but at least my new house was going to have all new shiny things in it.

CHAPTER FOUR

NOVEMBER

November came, and I didn't seem any closer to getting a house. I was just left here to languish, and I was getting desperate. Sometimes this place was bearable, at least that is what I had convinced myself, and I got on with pretty much everyone. I was such a fixture now that Pam, Sandy and Linda would all tell the new women to chat with me if they needed help. I didn't mind, I liked to help new ladies to settle in, even if many would be gone within days, sometimes hours. They probably took one look at the bunch at the kitchen and thought better of it.

Every now and then, we would get a resident that we found hard to tolerate. One being Janet's son, who was aged fifteen and was taller than most women in here. At his age, he was considered a child, but he was trouble. He had been here for stints before, but now he was living here permanently. Janet had absolutely no control over the little bastard. He basically sauntered around the place like he owned it, swearing, smoking, calling the small kids names and pushing them around. As a child, there were no punishments, just 'support'. However, I'm pretty sure that everyone at some point or another had complained about this scally, and I actually think that hard-faced Janet was a little ashamed, or I'd like to think she was. I would be.

The building had stone stairwells at each end, and one of these had double doors at the bottom. This was his favourite hideout. We used it to store buggies, but he used it as a den. Kids were too scared to go that way, but mums didn't always have a choice, and besides, why should people live in fear in a 'safe house'?

He cornered Mary when she was seven months pregnant. Clearly bullying the vulnerable was his thing. He held a knife to her stomach and told her he was going to stab the baby. This was an out of control teenager who was twice her size. However, Mary was not easily scared. When it came to 'fight or flight', Mary did both. She ranted and screamed at him to daze and confuse him, then got the hell out of there. She was shaken, and raised hell about the incident, and quite rightly too. This monster had to go. I knew the staff were trying to find him somewhere, but he was hell-bent on being as nasty as possible.

One day, Mary asked me to get her something from her room, and there he was waiting in the stairwell, it was standoff time. He didn't even say anything to me. He just held the door closed to trap me in. I could have gone the long way around to the other stairwell, but I opted to stand my ground. I asked him to move, and that wasn't happening, so I pulled the door open with such force that I nearly broke the little shit's wrist. I had a lot of adrenaline pumping, but I didn't hurt him. It's not my style to hurt kids, but I did want him gone, and luckily, he was removed from there a few days later. Janet seemed relieved too.

I soon learned though that when one villain leaves, another enters. Tracey was a young mum of twenty-two, and she had a son who was two, around a year older than Luke. I thought it would be great for my son to finally have a friend closer to his age, as he would get bored.

Tracey was the type of mum who always seemed to be trying her best but wasn't quite there. She seemed overwhelmed with motherhood. The biggest thing I picked up on was her obsessive need to gossip. My God, everything was a drama, and everything was exaggerated. I don't know if she wanted sympathy or if she wanted to shock people. I couldn't work that out, and I felt that something was off about her. I really did get warning signals that made me cautious. Tracey made friends easily as I think people liked her drama as it distracted women from their own stuff.

I always called bullshit, but I kept that to myself. It would have seemed like it was an issue, and I didn't want to be dragged into that drama. So, for the time being, I just had to watch people hang on her every word, and leave it be. She wasn't doing anyone any harm.

* * *

Around the middle of the month, I began to feel weak. I had lost my appetite and became very tired. I must have had a viral infection, but I couldn't go to the doctor as there was no one to look after Luke. I just thought I'd ride it out.

As I became worse, I asked Gina if she would mind watching Luke. She loved kids, and Luke liked her. But that went down like a lead balloon, and Gina became flustered and darted off. I thought it was a bit odd, and I went back to bed for a bit. I started getting worse and managed to drag myself to the office and asked for a doctor to be called, but they didn't as Pam said callouts weren't allowed. I was thinking, fine, I'll go back to my room and die then. But they did want to politely make me aware that I wasn't to ask Gina to babysit, under any circumstances. Erm, OK, then. That's all I was getting. I couldn't understand it, but, hey ho.

I had to ask Janet to pick the kids up for me as I had got to the point where every move I made caused exhaustion, pain, and I was wiped out. The other women all joined forces to watch the kids in the kitchen, feed them and send them in at bedtime. I knew there were women in there that I didn't really want to look after the kids, but I had no option. I couldn't move, I was hot, dripping with sweat and hurt everywhere.

Then I had an unlikely hero, Sadia entered my room with water and cool flannels. Nothing was said about our previous disagreement. She just became my Florence Nightingale and nursed me until I was better. She told me she would get me a hot toddy, but she came back with cold orange squash, and I was too weak to question it

The staff didn't seem to care. They came in once to make me sign for my mail and then left me to it. It was five days before I could get out of bed, and I spent weeks drained and exhausted. Whatever the hell it was, it had taken it out of me.

I suppose I was thankful, though as I had lost a lot of weight. I didn't realise it at first and had momentarily convinced myself that I had a lump. I was lying flat in bed, and I had an itch under my breast, and I felt a big hard lump. At that moment, I thought the illness I had was cancer. Then I realised it was my rib cage. I had lost so much weight. I was bony, and I hadn't felt my ribs for years. Panic over. I felt stupid yet relieved at the same time.

Most of November was consumed with illness. I used this new weight loss to kick start a healthier diet.

I'd been overweight since giving birth to Ellie, and it had served me a purpose. But that wasn't self-serving anymore, and I wondered what I would look like as a thinner person. I began planning meals better, and I couldn't believe I hadn't thought of this before. I certainly had the time to plan and shop and cook. There was, however, the little issue of the kitchen being packed at teatime with mums cooking, and the shared utensils being used, but that was OK, I would work around it.

Anyway, I had to get my strength back. My muscles were still weak, so I had to improve my health. The kids could still have their chicken nuggets and chips. The girls wouldn't eat anything that started with veg and ended with able. I would feed them at teatime and then feed myself after they had gone to bed.

Sandy was coming into the kitchen a lot during the day, checking on me. Sadia told me she had been asking everyone if they had seen me eat. They thought the weight loss was due to an eating disorder. Hello! Illness! I mentioned it. Remember? How nice to know they cared!

I was going full pelt. I went to the office and found a book on callisthenics, which I'd never heard of before. But it was a health book, so therefore it was my new companion. I would drop the kids at school then go back to my room and exercise, and then I would do the same at the kids' bedtime. I wasn't altering that much on the outside, but I felt stronger and more able at my core.

My clothes were getting loose, but nothing that a belt couldn't fix. I was used to oversized jumpers anyway. Sadia told me I needed new clothes, but I didn't have that much money. If I did have money, it was going on bits for the new house or nice things for the kids. Janet told me that there was a fund that you could apply to for new clothes. I thought that was great. Off I popped to the office to find out more. Janet was right, but unfortunately, you could only get a clothes' grant if you had put on a lot of weight, not if you lost weight. They reasoned that you could take clothes in, but you couldn't let clothes out—what a backward rule. Who the hell made that one up? Surely quick weight loss was more of an immediate need than weight gain. People spent years eating to acquire a larger figure, as it was more gradual. Oh well.

Sadia decided we needed a trip to the charity shops, and she wouldn't take no for an answer. That day changed my whole perspective on my self-image. Sadia was picking up jeans and tops that were obviously too small but demanded I try them on. I did, just to make a point to her that my fat ass was not getting into a size ten. At that point I cried, I was in a size ten pair of jeans, and even though they were tight as I had some loose skin due to my rapid weight loss, I was in them. I hadn't even known what size I was before. I bought everything in a size eighteen, even if it was big, because I felt like a size eighteen. When I walked into this shop, I felt like a size eighteen, but as I left, I felt thinner. I didn't feel like a ten, I was still a fat person, and my thighs were still tree trunks, but I had more shape. I had Sadia to thank for all this.

* * *

What was wrong with the kids in this place? I didn't like them. In fact, a few months here had made me hate other people's kids. My kids were amazing; they held me together. But other kids were just bratty, dirty little shits who crapped on floors, broke toys and were abusive to other kids.

Tracey's little cherub was no exception. He was constantly pushing Luke over in the garden, and as soon as he thought no–one was looking, he would shove him. I would tell Tracey, with a nicey-nicey, forced smile.

"You can't do that sweetie, say sorry to Luke," Tracey would say and that would be it.

That was fine. She was letting him know that his behaviour wasn't acceptable, best to make them aware at this age. However, it didn't stop, and it was becoming a daily thing. Part of the induction here was having a little chat about kids. Sandy had made me aware that kids see things at home. They often watch Daddy hitting Mummy, or putting her down and controlling her, and the children think this is normal behaviour. Then there are children who are abused by Daddy, and this can cause them to have their own issues too, as well as lashing out at other children. I got all that, and if the parents were supporting their children, then that was a great thing. But not all mums could take care of themselves and the kids or vice versa, and kids in here were damaged.

I had always tried to keep the kids away from any conflict with their father. I wasn't the argumentative type. Hence, screaming matches were not a fixture in their lives, and most of the time, he would disappear until the kids were in bed anyway. He only ever wanted it to be just the two of us, the kids got in the way. They served a purpose for him, they kept me pregnant and barefoot. Still, they inconvenienced him, and he was jealous of them. I was very maternal, but I'd planned on two, not so early, but it happened.

Once I had Ellie, I knew I wanted Nicole almost straight away so I could get a career going once they went to school. So that's what I did. Once Nicole was four, I somehow managed to land myself a job managing a small shop in the city centre. I'd worked hard to build a CV and even though I wasn't working, I had worked voluntarily and studied bookkeeping, so it impressed prospective employers, and it worked.

I had my start date, began my induction and training, and I was enjoying my sense of accomplishment. But then I was soon to discover I was pregnant again. This was the same thing that happened with Ellie. I got offered a great job and found myself pregnant - only Nicole was planned.

That man had always insisted on withdrawal as contraception, and it worked for years until I fell with Ellie, and years later, I fell with Luke. He had total control over whether I got pregnant. With Ellie, I thought there had been an accident, and he convinced me I was being stupid. With Luke, I didn't have a clue, but he told me it was deliberate as there was no way I was working in the city, and that was that.

I don't know if it was the male hormones raging around in me from carrying a boy, but I was so different this time. I was fed up of his crap, and I started standing up to him. He didn't like it, and he soon became more and more physical with me, more pushing, pinning me against walls, and more spitting in my face. I still wasn't conforming so he came up with a new plan. He wanted us to buy our council house. It was dirt cheap because of the length of time we'd lived there. I'd always wanted to get on the property ladder, and this was perfect because the value would triple after three years. The house was next to a great school, and the children had lots of friends there. He used this to pacify me for the last bit of my pregnancy. It was happening so I set to with nesting. I laid floor tiles in the dining room. I did ask him to help, but he didn't want to. I was used to that. Being eight months pregnant wasn't an excuse for laziness after all.

When I had Luke, I swore always to protect him. The beautiful, loving energy coming off this boy was immense, and I don't just think I was meant to protect him. I think he was gifted to me to help me too.

I had lost a huge amount of blood during pregnancy, and I was pretty exhausted from it. My mum had come to stay for a couple of weeks to help with Luke, and *that man* was all sweetness and light. He was helpful, he hoovered – weird, and he couldn't do enough for my mum, which was odd, as she absolutely hated him.

I momentarily thought he had grown up a bit. I had been standing up to him, and maybe he realised he had to be a better husband. But once the time came for my mum to leave, there he was, the twat was back. Upon waking in the night, I asked him if he could feed Luke.

"You wanted the little bastard. You look after him."

Whoaaaa there! Be as horrible as you want with me, but don't ever be nasty to a newborn baby.

It became evident over the next few months that he was jealous of our baby, even more than the girls because this was a boy, a competitor for male dominance. He didn't want anything to do with him. He refused to even accept him as his own. *That man* had always accused me of cheating. I don't know when I ever had time to cheat, because he was in charge of my time. I couldn't do anything without his consent, but nonetheless, I was sleeping with every man I came across, even his brothers. Then eventually I was accused of sleeping with my own brother, his mind was that twisted.

I knew that something had to change. When Luke was seven months old, our estate agent came around with the papers, the actual 'sign on the dotted line' papers. Once our signatures were on that paper, that was it, we would be homeowners. So, I set to, pen in hand, and couldn't sign it. I knew there was too much control in this relationship, if I had a house with him, I would never be free, and Luke deserved better. So, I refused to sign and asked both the estate agent and *that man* to leave.

* * *

Luke was now twenty-one months old, and he literally kept me sane. He followed me around like a little duckling and was always smiling. I swear he was sent to get me through all of this. I had to keep him smiling. I didn't want this place to tarnish him in any way.

The issue with Tracey's son was getting out of control. After yet another shove, I confronted her, at tea-time, in the packed kitchen, and I asked her to keep a better eye on him. That was like a red rag to a bull. Off she stormed to the patio area, picked up her boy, brought him in and clacked him full pelt on the bum.

"There!" she screamed, "Are you fucking happy now?"

Well no, I would have been happy if a member of staff had witnessed it, they would have thrown the bitch out. The kitchen fell silent. It wasn't even my kitchen, so I left them to it. Thank God, I could stay in my kitchen and not see her dramatic screwed up face. I felt so bad for her boy, and she would have loved the attention and the drama. But I was not going to go near her, and Luke was definitely not.

Now I had lost a lot of weight, Lisa decided to give me a proposition.

"Come and dance at my club," she said.

Erm, I don't think I was ready to show flesh, and besides, I was still fat. Lisa said she would help me, teach me some dance moves, and lend me some outfits. She said that men like girls of all shapes and sizes and assured me that I was good enough to be a lap dancer. Lisa was a natural at posing in a sexy way, and she showed me some warm-up dances. There was no way I was that bendy, and my memory was not good enough to remember what she was pulling off. But again, she assured me I would be great.

She came over one afternoon with some outfits, they were like slutty bikinis, and I felt so uncomfortable. For a start, Lisa was around a size six to eight, and I was a ten to twelve. She said they were stretchy and would fit me. So, I tried on a little lilac number, it was tight all right, and my fat hung out everywhere. I was still hiding saggy skin in my jeans, but it was starting to snap in a little. I was young and was working out, so it was getting better. But once Lisa re-entered the room and saw my hideous body, I think she changed her mind about my suitability. She never said it, but she also never spoke of it again. The offer just vanished. But it was OK, and I'm not sure if I could have done it anyway. You have to know you're sexy to do that, and I was anything but.

But I was starting to gain some confidence, and with Lisa's help, I was thinking about my clothes and my hair. We still had our little girly sessions, and Lisa was starting to rub off on me. I bought a velour tracksuit for the first time in my life, it was mint green, and I bought nice white pumps to go with it. My girls also got velour tracksuits - pink and purple. They were plain because they were from the market, but Lisa's was Juicy Couture because she loved her brands. For the first time in over six years, I was showing a bit of shape and not covering it up. Lisa was teaching me about hair extensions and make-up. I couldn't afford the extensions and had no intention of spending an hour a day putting make-up on, but I was painting my nails and dyeing my hair. There was only so long that a person could spend time with a scouser before being influenced by their style and habits. However, I decided against putting Luke in a tracksuit. I was not crossing that line.

* * *

Lisa became a good friend, and I was becoming more of a girl. I never had problems putting Ellie and Nicole in dresses or doing their hair nice, but I had never bothered with myself. One weekend, Lisa said I could go and stay with her at her boyfriend's house. I thought it would be a nice chance to have some proper girly time together. We went shopping for food for our tea, and we bought hot chocolate for the kids. It was great to have a night away from the bleak house.

It started well until Lisa said 'they' wanted her to work. I wanted to believe that, but I think she had planned for me to babysit all along. I obviously agreed to stay there with the four girls, and off she went. Whether it was work, or on a night out with her boyfriend, I'm not sure, I only saw him fleetingly anyway.

But still, I did enjoy the night away, and Lisa promised to make it up to me. So, she arranged for us to go on a night out in the city centre and would ask her mum to babysit the girls. I wasn't keen on a stranger looking after the children, so I contacted my parents and asked them to have the children instead. My dad wasn't sure at first, not because he didn't want the kids there as they used to stay there lots before I moved here, but he was worried that the idiot would be watching the house, and would cause trouble for me. I was so desperate to do something exciting that I convinced my parents that it was fine and we were going out in a couple of weeks. It was a long journey back home on public transport, but I knew it was going to be worth it.

I felt like I had something to look forward to. It was strange; it was just a night out. But with new people coming and going in here, the dynamic would change all the time. There were times I could escape the bleak house by going to Vic's for a coffee or a play date. I had someone to go shopping with most times. I was looking at clothes more and more, and I even bought myself a pink suede style jacket with a massive fur collar. I had never had a style before, it was nice to have something special for me.

I wasn't great at it though. I asked Sadia to help me find something nice for a night out. We were back in the charity shop, and she came across a sequined white tiger-striped vest top. It sparkled, and it was so cute but a bit revealing. I tried it on, and I felt amazing. My arms were getting thinner, my belly was getting flatter, and I had a good cleavage which I'd never wanted to show before. I was sold. I got a pair of black pants, which were slimming, and some heels - kitten ones. God, baby steps, I wasn't ready for high heels yet, I'd have been like a new-born giraffe. But I was set for when the time came, and I was going to be sexy!

Most of the time, the evening bunch were in my kitchen, and I didn't mind, because the other kitchen was weird. I could never get a good vibe in there, and it felt like our kitchen was the happy one while the other felt more oppressed and sombre. I didn't like it in there at all. Another reason was Tracey. It was her kitchen, and she and Janet were getting closer so they would be in there more.

One evening, most of the women were in there. I found this strange, so I scuttled in there to see what was going on. Tracey was upset, not with tears, but with drama. Janet told her to tell me all about it, like I would care. Tracey said she had breast cancer. So yes, I did feel a pang of sadness for her. She stood up and whipped her top up.

"Look, you can see the size difference. Look how different they are."

I wasn't expecting that, but it was clearly an emotive time for her, and I had to accept that I had been shown her boobs without wanting to actually see them. Yes, they were different sizes, but I wasn't a doctor, so I didn't know what to think. But she had been given a diagnosis of breast cancer and was seeking support. We were all behind her. There was a chance she could die, and her poor son would be left without a mother. I knew she was a drama queen, but this was one time that she was owed the sympathy. I felt so bad for her, and I couldn't dislike her knowing she had that going on. We all became her support network. We would do lots of things for her, sometimes babysitting so she could attend her appointments, other times being there with a wine. There were times when we would help her to pay for buses to the hospital. I saw a lovely side to this group of women. We were united in our care for her. It was a shame that she left a few weeks before Christmas. We clubbed together for a little leaving present for her, nothing much, just some flowers and pampering stuff. By God, she deserved it with the shit she was going through. That's why she wanted to be closer to her family down south. We were all eager to hear her how she was getting along, and Janet was the one who would keep in touch with her for us all.

CHAPTER FIVE

DECEMBER

I had always loved the run-up to Christmas because I loved anything sparkly. I loved Christmas lights and festive songs. I loved the idea of Santa and being caring and giving. But best of all, I loved the look on the kid's faces when they had their presents.

This year was no exception. I didn't care where we were. We were going to have a great Christmas. I bought a little decorated three-foot tree, lots of Christmas films from the flea market, and little Christmassy plates and cups. I was getting in the spirit, and no one would spoil it.

I was approaching my fifth month here now. I wasn't expecting to get the news of a house over Christmas and had accepted celebrating Christmas here - it was what it was. The good news was that Gina had been offered a flat, finally. I was so pleased for her. The single women generally waited much longer for a house than those with kids, so it had been a long haul for her—what a great Christmas present!

I was always happy when someone got a house, but a little sad too. Nearly five months I had been waiting, I shouldn't still be here. Three to four months, they said. I knew I couldn't be here indefinitely, but it was starting to feel like home, and that was a very bad thing. The bleak house was just so familiar now, and the weeks were so long that I was forgetting my old life. It felt like I had friends here, with the same bunch of women around the table at night.

My biggest worry was that I was getting used to my mind, I was still acting, and it was becoming normal. Inside I had a heavy heart, a black mind, and an indescribable emptiness. The reason that I felt so at ease around the table was because I wasn't alone. Being in my room at night meant I was in the presence of my inner demons, and they were waiting for me to break. I was hiding all this emotion, from the staff, the women, and the kids. I realised that I had become something that I hated, a control freak. I wasn't bossy with anyone else, but I controlled my emotion and my mind, and I wouldn't let anything out. I knew if I were to allow myself to feel anything at all, then it would all flood out of me and I would, at best, be committed. My children had to be protected from foster care, so I had to remain in control. The woman that everyone saw wasn't really the woman that I was inside. It was all pretence.

I wasn't hiding my personality. I was kind, caring, fun, and empathic. I did genuinely want good things for these women. I was happy when they had good news, and I really was looking forward to Christmas. Especially as it helped to fill about a hundredth of this void in me. But the women also thought I was super laid back, always smiling, really sociable, and I always had an empathic ear. There were women in here that didn't talk to anyone else but me. Gina had been one, so was Lisa. She never mingled with anyone else. Before Vic left, she had been all motherly with everyone, now that role seemed to be mine.

* * *

My brother had agreed to pick up the children and take them to their grandparent's house for the weekend. Oh my God, it was strange not to have them. Before I had moved here, they had spent a weekend every month with their grandparents. Their nanny had always wanted me to be able to have time for myself, but she secretly just wanted to have the kids to herself for a couple of days.

I knew I was lucky as I didn't have anyone in my friend group who had that luxury. My mum was rare, in that sense. I felt free, not to release emotion, because that was not going to happen, but free like I could do anything now. I couldn't believe I was having a night out, my first one since landing in this place. Going out was not a new concept to me. I had been single for a whole year before moving here, and boy, did I have some nights out. I had racked up some terrible memories from them, but I was out regardless.

Going out back home was always a challenge. I had my parents, and I had my nieces, so finding a childminder was never an issue. However, being stalked by an ex-partner was making it very difficult.

Nights out were generally with my sister or one of my best pals, Carrie, who had recently become single also. As soon as I became single, my friends wanted me to go out. I was never allowed to when I was married, not unless it was local, he was with me, or he approved of the friends I was out with. Basically, I went out about once every couple of years to the Local, though he would take himself out all of the time. Now I was single, I was going to enjoy it. I'd been in that relationship since I was sixteen years old, and I had never done the club scene.

Carrie and I had some of the best nights out. We drank a lot of vodka, we danced on tables, and we had a lot of attention from men, especially Carrie, as she was a blonde bombshell with a naughty glint in her eye. My God, *that man* hated her. He believed she was influencing me - she wasn't. I was loving the madness. Truth be told, I needed her, and she needed me. We had both just come out of long-term marriages, and we needed to go a bit mad. We always had each other's back, and we were safe. I soon started realising that there were some good-looking men out there it was a revelation.

That man was not a looker. He would always tell me women were chatting him up, and I believed him. But the only thing he had was a big set of blue eyes. The rest was meh! I didn't consider myself to be particularly good looking, even though I had gone through my teens attracting some good-looking boys and had never been called ugly by anyone other than that man.

Strangely, the entire time I was married, I never noticed other men. I don't know if it was because of my loyalty to my husband, or because it would cause me trouble to even glance at another man, but I just never fancied anyone. He would often stare at women, telling me they had nice tits, or they were gorgeous. He was always comparing me, trying to make me jealous, but it never worked. It did backfire, however. One day, when I picked a random man who was jogging past, I made a deliberate effort to say what a nice ass he had. That man didn't speak to me for a week.

Once I became single, my eyes suddenly became open. I would walk to the shop and see a handsome man, woo woo, eye candy. This was happening all the time. There were fitties everywhere. Going out with Carrie was like being a kid in a sweet shop. When I went out, I dressed in the same black pants, black long-sleeved top, hair in a bun and only wore mascara and lipstick, and yet I attracted a lot of blokes. I became hooked to this feeling. I craved going out so I could get chatted up. I knew in my heart of hearts that blokes only chatted up women because they wanted a shag, but I still enjoyed their effort. If I went home without being chatted up, it put me in a right mood, like I hadn't had my fix. I realised I was becoming a little addicted to going out. I was definitely going off the rails, drinking too much and acting like a whore to get men to chat me up. As much as I loved the attention, I knew men had one thing on their mind, and I was just using them to get my confidence hit. I never had any illusions of meeting a prince, and to be honest, I didn't want one. Men were saps to be used.

Carrie and I used to sometimes invite men back, where I could quite often talk the back legs off 'mine' for hours. My saps were unlucky, but I didn't think anything of it because I'd never promised them anything. Unfortunately, I did get the odd idiot who would call me a tease, a bitch, or whatever else. So what! I'd had what I wanted from them, those chat-up lines, and they'd expired their purpose.

I had a terrible end to a night when my sap for the evening got a bit angry. I wasn't heeding to his advances, and I didn't fancy him either. He didn't have any snogging action as I had made it clear he wasn't getting any. I was worried he was going to get aggressive, so I asked him to leave, and luckily, he did. He stormed out without his mate, who was getting lucky with Carrie upstairs.

I decided to prepare to bed down on the sofa when the front door flew open. I shouted, "I told you to fuck off." But it wasn't the sap. It was *that man.* He had messaged me earlier in the evening saying he wanted to see me. I had told him no, I was out. He demanded to know where I was, and I told him I was with Carrie and that I was going to be out until midnight. Midnight came, and I hadn't returned home, so he parked outside Carrie's and waited. He saw us going into the house with the two men. He waited until the man left, and realising the door was left open, he barged in screaming and shouting that I was all the sluts under the sun. Carrie came down and told him to get out, and the other bloke darted off. I was then dragged by my hair, kicking, and screaming to his car. I broke free and ran around to the back of the car where I punched the rear light twice, smashing it. I knew this car was his baby, and I wanted to hurt him. It definitely worked. he then grabbed me and threw me across the pavement, and I literally bounced. I was then shocked, and I couldn't move for several seconds. Everything seemed to fade out for a second, then the lights and sounds of the situation came back into focus. Then came the pain and the blood.

Carrie picked me up and pulled me into her house, he followed. My elbow was fucked up. It was covered in blood, the skin had been scraped off, and the bone was showing. Carrie wanted to call an ambulance, but he wouldn't allow it. He told her to patch me up, which she did. I was crying and sobbing, but he wouldn't leave. He was staying there to make sure that we didn't call the police. He perched himself on the chair and pretty much oversaw the whole night until dusk when I agreed to leave with him with the promise that neither Carrie nor I wouldn't report him. Carrie told me the next day that her neighbours had taken his number plate and description if I wanted to go to the police, but I knew that wasn't an option. He'd already told me he would go to social services and tell them I was a bad mum, and although I knew I wasn't, I also knew how convincing his lies had been over the years, so they would probably believe him. I covered my arm with long-sleeved tops so that no one would ask what had happened.

* * *

It was time for my first night out in over six months. I'd had a long enough break to change my attitude toward men. I still didn't want one, but I didn't want to use them to make me feel good either.

Lisa and I went to her mum's, where her girls were staying, and we got ready there. I was getting quite excited. This was going to be great until Lisa told me that 'they' had called her in. Again! All was not lost, however, as her brother Gary was there, and he would go out with me. I didn't even know her brother, but I wanted a night out, so I agreed to go. I pretty much treated him like a girl-mate, but I was stupid not to realise that I had been set up on a date. We drank and danced and once we hit the club, I realised that he liked me. He was sweet enough, though a bit of a drip, and he was definitely cramping my style. The drunker I got, the more I realised that he was stopping me being chatted up. I took matters into my own hands and started drifting off in a different direction on the dance floor. I was soon being chatted up by a man that wasn't a drip.

Although I was flattered that Lisa thought I was good enough fodder for her brother, I was enraged too as I did not want to be tied to anyone, especially on a night out. Gary managed to find me and started hovering around, and I was not happy. When asked if I was out with him, I stated that I was, but it was OK as he was my gay best friend. I realised quickly what a horrible, despicable thing that was when they began calling him queer and threatening him for being a bender. Gary, of course, didn't understand what was going on, but soon worked it out. He was aggressively bullied out of the club. I followed but lost him. I went back in, and this guy and his mates found me, trying to pick up where he'd left off with charming me, I shouted a few choice words and left them to it.

I'd never experienced gay-bashing before, and it was my entire fault. I was an absolute bitch. Carrie and I had always said we were lesbians if we wanted to lose men who were flirting with us, so I didn't see it as a big thing. How wrong was I? I felt so bad. It was sobering, and I decided to get a taxi back to Lisa's to apologise, but no one would answer the door, so I had to go back to the bleak house. I never saw Lisa again, or the hair straighteners, make-up and clothes that I'd left at her mums. I never got the opportunity to say sorry to Gary. That was something I would never do again.

I realised that when I had booze, I was a slut and a nasty person. I'd do anything for a bit of attention, and I needed to stop that. Lisa must have thought I was a nice person to want to hook me up with her brother, how wrong she was. In fairness, I thought it was unfair of her to sneakily set me up, considering where we lived it was a given that I didn't want a boyfriend. In the sobering light of day, I realised that what I did was pure mean, and hadn't previously considered myself to be a nasty person. I was genuinely shocked at what I'd done and that thought haunted me for a long, long time. I vowed after that that I would never do that again, and I would not drink so much on a night out.

It made me look at my character. I realised that I was broken, and I wasn't holding it together as I thought. I had real issues when it came to men. I would listen to stories from the other women and listen to them saying that all men were bastards, and they were all the same. I didn't believe that. I thought there must be some nice guys out there, or at least I hoped there were. I knew that I wasn't interested right now, but eventually I believed that I would want to have my happy ever after. Then I'd catch myself and tell myself that I didn't need a man to complete me, I would stay single until I was fixed, and I knew exactly what I wanted in a relationship, no matter how long that took. Yep, I was going to be an old maid!

* * *

I was used to feeling nothing. This guilt was not pleasant, and I had to try and move on from it. I was going to work on myself, get some self-help books or something, and try to be more positive. The new year would be my new start, and I was going to be a different person. But first I had Christmas to look forward to. That was my focus.

With Lisa moved out, and Tracey and Gina gone, there was room for more new women. This place was nearly always full. It was never more than a couple of days before a room was occupied. The downside to new women coming in was when they moved people around. I had the largest room by far, but in fairness, I had the most kids. No one else ever had more than two. Every now and again, they would ask me if Luke was still using the cot. They asked this because they were trying to move me to a smaller room, and I would say yes. Actually, Luke slept in my little single bed with me. If he was going to sleep on a metal bed with a plastic mattress and quilt, then he could sleep in my bed. Luke had had some evenings where he couldn't settle.

All in all, he was a very placid baby. I never had trouble with him, until one evening he was teething quite badly and screamed for hours. Sandy kept checking on him as my room was right next to the office. I seriously thought they were checking to see if I was abusing him. I couldn't calm him at all, and I thought that they would get social services. I panicked at every little thing to do with the kids. I lived in constant fear of them being taken away from me. I had been made paranoid by *that man*.

In the year that I remained in my home after our separation, he had repeatedly told me he would report me to social services. It was his tool to make me comply. On two occasions, he did report me. The first time was to the police, who reported it to social services. He had been to my house to talk to me, and I refused to let him in, so he kicked the front door in and broke the lock. Due to it being Friday evening, the council wouldn't fix it until Monday, so I had to keep it closed as best as I could and go about my business.

On the Saturday, I was going to enjoy a night in my Local with my sister, and my babysitter was watching the children while we got ready. Unbeknown at the time, a gust of wind had blown open the front door and Luke had got out and managed to get onto the path outside. By all manner of coincidence, that man's nephew happened to be walking past and brought him back in. My sitter told me what happened, and I secured the door further. I decided I was still going out as there was no harm done, and I was putting Luke to bed before I went out, so he was not going to get out again.

My sister and I left, began the five-minute walk to the pub when along comes that man screeching to a halt in his car. He was raging and saying our son could be killed or kidnapped while I was out, and he was going to the house to take him as I was not fit to be a mother. My heart was burning. I raced back to the house and stopped him. He, of course, called the police, and they came to check on the safety of the children. They said they had no concerns. They understood that vengeful partners could make reports of this nature and assured me that although it had to be reported to social services that I shouldn't worry too much.

It wasn't long before the police were there again, this time because he had set up a situation to land me in trouble. I knew that he didn't want to see the children, but I also promised I would never stop him from seeing them. I was taken aback when he said he wanted to spend some quality time with them, so I arranged for him to come to the house to see them. I didn't feel that he was going to take them, and when he indicated that I could use the time to go shopping, I leapt at the chance. I was obviously not as long as he thought I'd be, as I managed to foil his set up. He left them home alone, a six-year-old, a five-year-old, and a one-year-old. He left them there so he could tell the police that they were by themselves and that I'd left them there. I arrived home just before the police got there, and I told them everything. There was nothing they could do, as the children hadn't been found alone, but there was strike two, another report to social services. One more and I knew I'd be investigated thoroughly.

I was so angry, and I asked him what the hell he was doing. He acted dumb, saying he had popped to the shop to get some treats for the kids, and hadn't called the police. He did use it to his advantage, though. I believed that there was a real risk of my children being taken away from me, and he was using them to make me do what he wanted. He had no qualms about calling the police again or setting me up if I didn't play along. He told me he wanted me back and that he was going to ruin my life if I didn't take him back. I had to play smart. There was no way I could have this monster in my life. He was winning the battles, but I had to win the war.

* * *

The bleak house saw several residents come and go through December, but a few stayed. Beryl, a single woman of around forty, arrived taking Gina's room. Then there was Lynn and her three-year-old son to take Tracey's room. There was also a woman of around twenty-three with a toddler who took Lisa's room. Then finally, somewhere upstairs, was a much older lady. I'd say she was around sixty at a guess, but stress can be ageing, so I could have been way out.

The new women didn't know what they were letting themselves in for. My first days here were wrought with anxiety, but these new ladies had an awful welcome. Someone's psycho ex popped around to shoot at the windows. Luckily, the glass was bulletproof. I'm sure Sandy telling us this was supposed to be reassuring, but it wasn't. I wanted to know what the hell had happened in the past that had made them use bulletproof glass? I never found out the whole story, and all I could do was hope that it didn't happen again. What a Christmas present that would be. Stepping out and getting shot. I needed a break from this.

I'd decided to be brave and arrange to go and spend Christmas at my parents' house. I knew this would be a bit dangerous, but I seriously had to get away from here, and the kids needed a break. Just the thought of spending Christmas within these bland walls was unimaginable.

I had been busy buying presents and being as excited as I could be. But it wasn't about the day itself. It was more to do with the women who would be stuck here. The staff were going to make it special enough by paying for the ingredients to make a slap-up turkey dinner with the trimmings. But Christmas was always going to be a difficult time for the families, with memories raging, whether good or bad and the sense of emptiness that shouldn't be there on Christmas day. As much as I always listened to any woman who wanted to share, I didn't want to be around that much sadness at Christmas. It would have been too much to bear. I also knew that with new women came new heart-breaking stories, and watching these women adjust to this bleak place would also be sad.

I didn't get much opportunity to spend time with the women before I left for Christmas. I connected with Beryl, and we bonded so quickly. I didn't know why, but it may have been because of her age. She was quite close in age to my mother. Beryl also spent all of her time in the kitchen, and time in that kitchen was different to anywhere else. Bonding happened much more rapidly. Dislike could also occur abnormally here. Emotions, in general, came in stronger clusters between the women. Outside of this place, if you met a mum at the schoolyard, it would happen by catching their eye most mornings, then saying hi. You might then talk for a minute or two, here or there, and then eventually you find yourselves chatting for half an hour outside the gates. This would then move on to a coffee invite, followed by the slow method of bonding as you start to unravel yourselves over many coffees. Then playdates with the kids, meals out with the families, and girls' nights on birthdays and Christmas. Usually a long drawn out occurrence.

In the bleak house, you could know someone's deepest fears within a few days, their relationship patterns, how they deal with anxiety, whether or not they are an absolute bitch, all pretty quickly. In here, you bond over a couple of coffees, Lambrusco or knock-off vermouth pretty much straight away.

Beryl was larger than life. She had a very strong presence. I think Christmas was going to be better in there because of her being there. It wasn't just me who thought she was a great addition to the kitchen crew; we all did. I was going away soon, and I knew that things could change considerably while I was away. Some people came and went so fast. But I knew that Mary and Sadia would be here when I got back at least, and hopefully Beryl.

The bleak house usually had a strict rule about time away. They said that if you were never there, then you clearly had somewhere else to live and did not need that room that would be essential to someone else. For this reason, you weren't allowed out for more than two nights a week, and you also had to be in by 11pm. There was a three-strike rule to ensure compliance. During the holidays, this rule was discretionary, so I had been permitted to take a couple of weeks away. I was so happy to pack for some time in normality.

As I left, I was handed three big bin bags, one for each child. I received lots of age-appropriate gifts for the children and presents that had been donated by generous shoppers. When supermarkets make a plea for presents for disadvantaged children, a proportion of the gifts are given to children in refuges. I was absolutely humbled. These were all brand new toys for my kids from complete strangers with huge hearts. I actually felt like we weren't deserving. I felt some kids needed them more, and then I remembered the shit that my kids were facing every day by living here, and I knew they should have them. These gifts had been wrapped and divided into bags for every child in here, and I was particularly happy that the new ladies had gifts for their children, especially as they had to leave everything behind, just like I had almost five months ago.

Those two weeks spent with my family was just what we needed. I did have that niggle in the back of my mind that there was going to be an unwelcome visitor who would come and cause trouble, but I took some precautions. I arrived under cover of darkness, and I didn't leave the house, and the children didn't play outside. We stayed in a little bubble inside the house and didn't visit anyone, not even Zara or Carrie.

That Christmas was not as joyous as some of our previous Christmases. As much as I tried, I couldn't lose my black cloud, or be happy on demand. I had every reason to be in good spirits. I was free of my dictator. My children surrounded me, my parents and my siblings and their children were here. We had fabulous decorations, great food, and party games. It really was brilliant, but I felt so lonely and disconnected. These people were my family, they loved me, and I loved them. But I didn't feel like I had anyone in the world.

On that day, and many more to come, I felt like I was a person standing in a room watching other people living their lives, and I wasn't part of it, I was just an observer. From then on, I would always zone in and out of my own presence. That became my unwanted gift from Santa that year, and I couldn't hide it in the back of a drawer, I couldn't re-gift it, and I couldn't take it back to a shop. Thanks, Santa.

CHAPTER SIX

JANUARY

New Year came and went. I had made a resolution to try harder to get a house and to try to work on myself. The only problem with that was my lack of enthusiasm. I literally could not be bothered. It was all words. When it came to the kids, I could get my arse in gear. But if it was for me, then nada. The only thing that gave me a reason to be on this planet were my amazing children and getting them the house, and the life, that they deserved.

Beryl appeared to be a positive person with a bright outlook. She always seemed to know if the women needed some tea and sympathy, and she was always there, in the kitchen, on hand for any little drama that came along. She really was taking the mummy role from me, and I didn't mind one bit. I had kids to look after, whereas Beryl only had herself, and I imagined it was very boring for her. Looking after everyone gave her a sense of worth.

Beryl was quite a tall woman, she had wild, jet black, curly hair, dark freckles, her skin was brown but not very dark. Yet it was dark enough for her to refer to herself as 'this black ass'. She would say, 'This black ass is going to bed', and 'This black ass needs to hit the gym'. She also had a strong Welsh accent, so the phrase 'this black ass' sounded almost poetic.

Beryl wore sports clothes a lot. She loved her comfort. If it wasn't sweatpants, then it was pyjamas and a fluffy robe. She always made the place look more homely. I could imagine her in a country suite in front of a roaring fire. In fact, she had a type of grace that was slightly uppity, not in a snotty way, but in a way that showed that she expected nice things and was striving to have that kind of lifestyle.

Beryl was a sharer. She was happy to openly share her life and her teabags. She would show us pictures of her family and tell stories of her fallouts with her children, in particular her daughter. Beryl was here because she didn't get on with her daughter. She said her daughter was nasty and bullied her to the point where one of them had to go, and it was Beryl. She would recall stories of savage fights to the point where her daughter would hit her. It was quite sad. I knew domestic abuse was never as cut and dry as a bloke hurting a woman. But to have your daughter turn against you in that way was awful. I could never imagine falling out with my girls, especially to the point of physical altercations. My girls were so sweet. I couldn't understand how it had got to that point with Beryl, where she had to lose her home and her life to get away from her own daughter. That was never going to happen with my daughters. I would make sure of it. I guessed that Beryl would be in here for a while, as single ladies always were unless they went back to their partners.

Usually, January would be the sort of month that would have some little sparks of newness and hope. This month didn't have any of that, but we were told that we were having brand new kitchens, and the whole building was going to be repainted. Yippee! Not. This meant that there would be headache-inducing paint smells, lots of banging and dust. On top of that, the whole building would be sharing one kitchen while they took turns with the fitting. And to top it all off, as Luke was about to turn two, they told me I had to move to a smaller room.

They told me someone was moving in who needed that room, but they wouldn't give me details. I had begun to acquire quite a few bits here, including house stuff and clothes, so we had a lot to shift. I hoped it would fit in a smaller room. The upstairs room had two sets of bunkbeds, quite close together, and had some floor space between them and the door, so we weren't totally caved in.

As Luke always slept with me anyway, I allotted one bunk for 'stuff'. I had pans, utensils, duvet covers, bathroom stuff, even a microwave. Technically, there was now nowhere for Luke to sleep but with me. I moved into the new room, and I moved all the drawings that I had on my wall that the children had done to brighten the place up. I decided that a change was as good as a rest. The other women helped me move, so I didn't have to make too many trips up and down those stairs.

I was pretty pissed off when a single woman moved into the room, then out again before the next afternoon without even speaking to anyone. If there had been a large family or a disabled woman who needed the ground floor room, then fine. But why move me for one woman to come and go like that? I wasn't happy about it. But there was nothing I could do or say. They had been trying to get me out of that room for ages now, especially Pam. She never liked me. I probably wasn't needy enough. Pam only ever came into her own with the truly sad cases, never with me. She hated me. She was always talking down to me, giving me looks and generally was never going to be a support to me. I just stayed away from the bitch. I told myself that wherever there were volumes of vulnerable people, that there were people who had a power rush and wanted to abuse that vulnerability. That was Pam. She had power over me, but I wouldn't play ball. She was nasty to me, but I couldn't stand up for myself because she would throw me out, and I hated her for it.

My new chores that I had to do daily were mopping the halls and cleaning the downstairs toilets. What the hell did I deserve to get this job? Was there any mother in this place besides me that taught their kids how to use a toilet? There was piss and shit all over the seat, floor, walls. It was vile! The toilet rolls never lasted either as they would be put in the toilet more often than not, or unravelled and peed on. What was wrong with these people? It was a terrible job, but then I had been in charge of the playroom before this, and that wasn't much better. But at least there would be the odd day where no one used that room, and I wouldn't find pee in the toy boxes.

Another problem with the room move was the bathroom sharing. Downstairs we had our own sink, but upstairs was fair game to all. It was crazy enough in the morning trying to get the kids ready without fighting for a sink. The worse part was that I wasn't competing with other mums. The new older lady, Miriam, pretty much kept herself to herself. But every morning at 8am she would go into a bathroom, usually mine, and take an hour-long bath. This meant that every morning we were all down by a bathroom. We complained to the staff. We complained to her. But she wasn't going to stop doing it. We had to get in there before her; it was the only way. I just wanted my kids to brush their teeth!

Could she not hang fire until nine? It wasn't like she had anywhere else to be. We would never even see her unless she was making a cup of tea. She wouldn't talk to anyone, so she set herself up to be judged. She was a weedy woman, with ashen skin, and she looked dull, like she had given up. But she wasn't here to make friends, and she was doing a good job of alienating herself, without ever saying a word.

Another woman who didn't say much was Lucy. She was around twenty-three-years-old and had a ten-month-old daughter. Lucy didn't connect that much. It wasn't because she was unfriendly, it was more that she was in shock at being here. The distress was continuously etched on her face. She looked like she was frowning even during normal conversation. We all carried our anxiety around, but Lucy really did wear it on her face. It was a shame too, as she had such a pretty face. She was a petite brunette, who didn't have an ounce of baby fat left on her, but I don't think she was a big eater anyway. Her daughter was adorable, so innocent. What had the poor darling been born into?

Whereas some women in here had been abused for years and were worn down with it, Lucy's abuse started in pregnancy. She had previously had a good relationship with her boyfriend so she couldn't believe that he turned abusive. With Lucy, she knew pretty much straight away that she had to leave. Even though she loved him, she didn't want her daughter to be hurt.

The distress was there on her face with the shock of her boyfriend turning like that hadn't sunk in yet. Why had he done that? I had a lot of respect for Lucy, and a lot of the other women here too. But she knew he was not going to go back to his former self, so she got help. It could be hard for a lot of women. They're manipulated and chipped away at until they don't have the strength, money, or the support to leave. Sometimes they genuinely think their partners will change.

Lucy got out of there, and I admired her. Lucy, in obvious distress, seemed to be hopeful. Like some of the ladies before her, she confided in me more than the others, and for the short time she was there, I was there for her. She used music as a tool for stress management. She listened to lyrics and could relate to them as if some songs had been written with her in mind.

A few weeks into January, Lucy was being moved to another refuge, and she wanted a clean start. She didn't have much family as her mum had passed away while she was young, which was why her daughter's wellbeing was so important to her.

Before she left, she gave me a CD. It was Cyndi Lauper's, Twelve Deadly Cyns. This was her favourite album, and she wanted me to have it as she said the music helped her through anything. I agreed as most of the words resonated, *'change of heart'*, *'who let in the rain'*, and *'the world is stone'*. Cyndi was hitting the nail on the head, and Lucy gave me an amazing gift. I hadn't known her long, but I missed her when she left and thought about her when I put on her Cyndi CD. Some women really did make an impact on me.

That bloody woman upstairs, Miriam, was getting on my nerves, but I wasn't the kind of person who would wish anything bad on people. That couldn't be said for everyone. I'd already seen, these women could act like a pack if they wanted to, I'd seen it with Meera. But then Miriam became a target, and the pack master was Beryl. I noticed that she would move Miriam's things around so that when she went to find them, they weren't there.

I saw her dropping her cutlery into the bin. I also witnessed her putting salt in her tea, and even dipping her cup into the toilet bowl. This was vile and juvenile, but I wasn't going to get involved. As much as I disliked Miriam, I didn't like what was happening with Beryl. But I was not going to open myself up as a target and have the pack turn on me.

I couldn't ignore it for long though, and I talked to Sandy about it. Sandy told me that she would not reveal my name but had to stop what was happening. It worked, and Miriam left. But Beryl was in a foul mood for days and was probably trying to work out who had grassed her up. I saw a side to Beryl that I wasn't keen on, but still, everyone liked her and would look to her for advice and leadership. She was a pack master. I just carried on as normal. I had enough friends in this place to not be worried about being a target without just cause. But I also knew that there was no such thing as loyalty here, so I decided to be cautious just in case. Beryl never told anyone why she had been in the office, or why she was in a bad mood, but I knew, and I tried to remain as aloof as I could when I was around her.

* * *

With all departures comes new arrivals. In came an eighteen-year-old girl with a two-month-old baby. The baby girl was a cutie, the mother, Ashley, not so much. This woman looked awful, and she was built like a brick shithouse. She wore a full tracksuit, bright white Air Max trainers, gold chains, and her bright red hair was scraped back, and I mean scraped. It looked painful. She had a round and completely expressionless face. If Miss Trunchbull had red hair and wore trackies, this would be her twin.

However, looks aside, she was here for a reason, and no one knew her story. I just couldn't take to her though. Maybe it's because she just lurked, and when she sat, she sat like a bloke, legs wide apart and back hunched over. It also could have been because of how long she would let her little baby cry before she tended to her. Ashley was in the kitchen most of the time, but she never really chatted, she was a closed book. She was just 'there'. It was very odd.

One of the better things to come from January was Mary's new baby boy, and it was about time too. She was huge and had seemed to be pregnant forever. It was a welcome distraction having this new baby here from one of our own. It was like the baby had a house of aunties. Mary, of course, had everyone running around after her, she had always done, so now was no exception. We all chipped in to help Mary. We loved cuddling the baby.

Mary didn't do that much. She was known for being lazy and dirty. Her room was the messiest in the building, and she had received warnings about it. Having a baby wasn't about to make her a clean person, and we 'aunties' did a lot of nappy changing and bottle warming for Princess Mary. We knew that the baby was loved though, and that counted for a lot. News of the baby also came with news of a house for them. It was brilliant news, especially as it was just across the road in Roughsville and it meant another place for me to escape.

Sadia was also going to leave soon. They were moving her to a house in an area which was deemed safe for her. I was getting worried, as all of the familiar faces were leaving. I had been here longer now than anyone I had known so far, so surely it couldn't be much longer for me. The staff were hopeful. They didn't know of anyone waiting this long to be housed, and Sandy was contacting agencies for me to try and speed them up.

Sadia and I had shared a lot of drinking around that kitchen table. We may have had a rough start, but we were quite close now, and I'd miss her. We decided that we would have a night out. There was still no one here to look after the kids, so I managed to get another weekender at the grandparents. This was going to be great. This night out was more for Sadia, as she hadn't been out for a long time, and she missed her hometown. I believed that the risk of her running into anyone she knew was small, so I had no concerns about us hitting her old haunts in the city.

Her kids went to her mums, and we had a really good girly night. I'd learned my lesson about drinking too much. I told myself spirits only, no mixing, and also I was going to stick to my girl pal like glue—no talking to men, no glancing at men, nothing.

Sadia and I had a lot of drunk chat, and I finally found out what had happened with her. I knew she had witnessed a murder, but what I didn't know was that it was an Arabian gang that was looking for her, to shut her up. And it got better; they were from this city. They would drink in the places we were in. I don't know what Sadia was thinking coming here, but she clearly was a one-woman act of rebellion. I think she had finally had enough of being told what she could or couldn't do, where she could go and where she couldn't. That was all fine, except I was now terrified.

"Don't worry," she assured me. "If I see any of them, I'll tell you to run."

My night hinged on her seeing them before they saw her, and I was not comfortable with that. I was constantly looking out for Arabian men, and it was distracting. The more I drank, the more I thought we were going to be murdered. I suggested that we should leave, but Sadia was having none of it. She was out, drinking her brandy and enjoying her freedom. I didn't want to take that away from her, so we continued on a wing and a prayer. The 3am taxi was the best one I had ever gotten into - the relief.

It was hard saying goodbye to Sadia a few days later, but I had her number, and she promised that I could go there for a night away once she was settled.

* * *

It seemed quite busy this month, what with Mary's move, and helping her to decorate. I was also still visiting Vic's as we were still close. People were just coming in and out really quickly this month. There had been so many countless women and kids here since I arrived. I was like a part of the furniture now. The staff never needed to check on me. I always did my chores, and my room was always clean on inspection days. I took part in all of the classes they had, and I had pretty much adjusted.

I had to get used to Mary not being perched at the end of the table, but Beryl soon took her spot. We all had to put up the with the upheaval of the kitchens being fitted, but it wasn't so bad, the men were eye candy. The worst part was having to use the other kitchen temporarily. I still felt so oppressed in there. It was dismal. I spent a lot of time with Mary thankfully, and I would get the kids a chippy tea after school and take it to hers.

The house had been left in a right state, so there was a lot of cleaning to be done. Mary's eldest boy had wanted a castle-themed room, so Beryl had offered to paint his room accordingly. Grey castle walls went nearly all the way up, then a blue sky with clouds. There were black windows and some green vines. It was hideous, and it was dark. Beryl was not a decorator and had ruined this room. I'm pretty sure the boy loved it, but it was horrid. Maybe a carpet would make it better, but Mary was waiting for a grant to come through, so the bare floors had to wait.

I hated that this house was so messy when there was a newborn baby here. Once the painting was done, I would go round there just to tidy. I knew Mary appreciated the help. Nothing changed here. Mary still wasn't looking after the children properly. They were dirty and pretty much fended for themselves. She did get food, but it was all frozen, and the kids had to microwave it themselves. She always gave them money for the ice cream van though, that was their little treat. The baby was fed, and his nappy was changed. It was just a shame that she always left the nappies on the floor. They would pile up, be kicked around when the kids were running, and then burst open until the contents would be smeared all over the floors. I couldn't sit there in that, so I would clean up. I was doing this pretty much every day. It got me out of the bleak house.

It wasn't long before Mary's boyfriend, the children's father, moved in. I soon realised that Mary had abused the housing system. She had wanted a move and got one. She had never mentioned this man before, and here they were playing happy families. He was a slob too, so they suited each other to a tee. I couldn't believe that Mary was one of 'those' pleading abuse to get a house, but I still wanted my escape pad. It was done now, but Mary was still making questionable decisions.

I waltzed around there one day to find she had a new puppy, a staffy, with a new leather harness. It was a beautiful dog, a blue, she said, whatever that meant. I was curious as to where Mary got the money for a puppy. I soon found out that it came from her grant for carpets. What an actual idiot. She spent money buying a dog, that money was supposed to buy carpet. I wasn't happy, but there was nothing I could do. The woman had a baby that was going to start rolling around on wooden floors with nails all around the edges. Even with this, I still went there most days.

Life in the bleak house stayed bleak. The staff asked me if I would consider counselling. I said I would, and they referred me. I'd never really understood what counsellors did, and I was pretty sure that there were others in here that needed that referral more than me. But I just carried on day to day while I waited for an appointment.

We had two very young and beautiful new residents, two sisters, one was eighteen and the other, just fourteen. They were such lovely young ladies, which was why their story was so tragic. The girls were Muslim and were running away from arranged marriages. The older sister was already married, and the younger sister's husband had already been chosen. Once the older sister had sought help, she had managed to get her sister away from the family, risking both of their lives. This was so horrific.

I was pretty naïve about some cultures. I didn't understand what went on. I'd never had reason to learn about different religions and cultures, so this was a shock. These two young girls had targets on their heads because they wanted to marry for love. They didn't stay that long. They had to move much further away as they were in too much danger here. I wondered how long those girls would be on the run for, and if they would ever get their lives back. These were just regular teenagers who wanted a normal life. It made me realise how much I took for granted with my right to marry who I chose. Even if it was a mistake, it was mine to make and not forced on me, well, not in that way anyway.

As a girl, I couldn't wait to get married. I didn't know who to, but I'd hoped I would find my prince. I only had one serious relationship before I met that man, so I wasn't experienced in settling down. My previous boyfriend finished with me for another girl, so I didn't have the best track record. I found myself pregnant within three years and was being told we were getting married. It wasn't a proposal; it was more of an order. I hadn't ever considered actually marrying this man. Sure we had been together three years; he had moved into my flat, and I was now pregnant. But marriage? I wasn't feeling it.

We had this conversation while walking through the local high street, where he told me we were getting married. I told him I didn't want to, and he made it clear that if I didn't marry him, he would leave me. With hindsight, that would have been a blessing. But he knew that I didn't ever want to be a single mum. He played on my insecurities and told me I would never cope on my own, that I'd be a terrible mother. I would never be allowed to keep the baby, and on top of it all that, I would shame my family. He really did hit me with it all. I'd told him early in our relationship that when I had kids, I wanted to be married, be settled, and bring kids into a secure environment, so he knew he could use this to get me to agree to marry him. And so I did.

There was no hen party, no big wedding, and no honeymoon. We wed in a registry office a few weeks later with a £10 dress off the market, surrounded by immediate family. My mum had put on a little buffet back at my parent's house. Yep, we went all out. My dream wedding was still a dream, but it was what it was. I did feel a little better that my kids were being born into a marriage, a family. It was still scorned upon to have kids out of wedlock, and I was doing it the right way, I'm not sure who it was right by, but still.

CHAPTER SEVEN

FEBRUARY

People were moving in and out so fast these days that my head was spinning. I also felt I was still embroiled in a breakdown. I would do anything for something normal, something fixed. I just wanted a home. It was hard sometimes visiting Mary and Vic and seeing them living their lives without these rules that could see them homeless.

Vic, especially, was house-proud. She was doing great. Her house was clean and carpeted. If this place had taught me anything, it was to never take things for granted, a home, a carpet, and curtains. Also, there were the other women. I pretty much got on with everyone, but that doesn't mean I liked them all, and I certainly didn't trust anyone. They could be parading as a friend but stealing and plotting behind your back.

Maybe I was exaggerating, but upon helping Mary with her laundry, I had noticed a pile of clothes that had gone missing from my own, Luke's clothes. She was obviously stockpiling a little collection there. I confronted her, and she said they were in the donations pile. I knew they hadn't been, but I still liked my messy sanctuary there, so again, I dropped it.

It was always manic here when we had a donations day. The whole kitchen table would be filled with bin bags full of second-hand clothes in all different sizes. It was first-come, first-served. However, these women were like a pack of animals. It was like a Next sale! It was even worse when there were kids' clothes in there. Donation days carried their own rules, and it was dog eat dog. I had gotten some great stuff. Beryl enjoyed a bit of order so she would try and command the table, especially if there was someone new who had a greater need. In my case, with my weight loss, Beryl would hoard a few bits for me before anyone had a chance to grab them.

These days were greatly received. The refuge itself couldn't stockpile donations because they would get rats. Once we were done, the bags were sent on to somewhere else. Sometimes it would be a donation of used toys. They would quickly go into the toy room. Anything decent would be stolen, and the rest would be broken. Toys did not last long here.

I wasn't counting the days of how long the kitchens took to finish, but they didn't take too long. Whilst they were being done, we had our little talks and classes in the much-underused living area. They had begun a new two-weekly class for residents and ex-residents to have a coffee and a meet-up. I really enjoyed it because it meant Vic and Mary would come over. There were also a couple of other familiar faces, but these two were my only constant.

The sessions were almost informal. There were some rules, such as not being allowed to talk about new residents or share things of a sensitive nature. I appreciated that rule. But I could just go to their houses and do it if I wanted to.

New ladies didn't really attend. They may have felt overwhelmed with the cliques already formed. I will always remember the day Vic was asked to leave and never return after making a comment about 'blackies' coming to the country. I found the term so derogatory that as soon as she said it, I looked at Sandy with a slightly gaping mouth. Sandy looked back at me. It was one of those disbelief moments. Sandy knew what I was thinking. This meeting was supposed to be a safe, non-judgmental, non-discriminatory space for all. Vic had now caused distress which meant that she couldn't take part anymore. I didn't want her there after that, anyway. I didn't see Vic much after that incident, just now and again she would come to Mary's for a catch-up.

We had a new single lady come in, Elizabeth. I would age her at around forty-five. She was slightly overweight, well dressed, with neat hair in a stylish up-do. Her demeanour was quite posh. She was closest to Beryl's age but came across mentally older. Whereas Beryl could speak to anyone, of any age, Elizabeth wasn't so confident. Either that or she was just not friendly. But her presence became more interesting when we discovered that she was a counsellor. She had definitely come into the lion's den here. We could all do with her, that was for sure.

Maybe that was why she became more reclusive as time went by. Being the longest-serving roomie here, I was friendly and spoke to her when I could. I had the odd coffee in her room, but she was a closed book. One day, she had two teenage boys come knocking for her. It turned out that they were her sons. They were living with their father and missing their mum terribly. I personally would have had them with me, but she was secretive so we could never be sure what was going on. These young men visited a few times, and they seemed like nice boys. It seemed so tragic that they were all split up.

The month of my birthday was finally here, and I decided to go out to the local city with my old pal Carrie and my sister. It had taken some arranging, a lot of secrecy as well. The children had pretty much resumed their monthly weekends at their grandparents, with either my brother or my father doing the pick-ups and drop-offs. Given the distance between us, the logistics had to be executed right. City nights out weren't cheap. It was my birthday, though, and we were missing each other. I had to have special permission to stay out later than eleven, but it was granted.

The problem with me drinking was that I didn't seem to know when to stop. I was also very friendly. I would talk to anyone, male or female. I was going to enjoy my birthday drinks and throw caution to the wind. I had no rules tonight.

We had a great night. Carrie gave me a beautiful silver necklace for my birthday, which I put in my coat pocket. As the birthday girl, I had several free drinks and attention from a very good-looking man. We talked for a while, and I found out he was a fireman. I always did like a fireman's uniform. I thought my luck was finally changing, but I couldn't stay there with him as our groups were going in different ways. I did get a birthday kiss, though, and I had his number.

I had no kids to get up with in the morning, so I could get hammered. I got so drunk that I had to be sick. I ran off to the ladies and spent a considerable amount of time hugging the toilet seat. When I finally had enough energy to get up and go back to the dancefloor, I realised I couldn't see my girls anywhere, or my bag, or my coat. I searched everywhere, but they were gone. I was known for chatting to guys so much that they maybe thought I'd left with one. Not that I would do that, but there had to be a reason for them to leave me.

Panic started kicking in. I was here in a big city, surrounded by drunk men, all alone, freezing, with no phone, no money, and no way to get back to the bleak house. I was still very drunk, and now crying my little heart out. I was desolate.

Eventually, a man approached me. I'd say he was around twenty-five. He looked friendly and had come to see if I was OK. He had a friend with him who wasn't keen on him talking to me and made that very clear. I told him what had happened, and he offered to take me to his home. He said he didn't have enough money to pay for a taxi for me, as he had not brought out his card. But if I were to go home with him, he would go to the cashpoint first thing in the morning and get me home. He seemed to really want to help, and I didn't have much of an option. His friend wasn't happy, but I got in a cab with them. He gave me his jacket, and he even stopped at the garage and bought me ten fags. The taxi dropped his mate off, and I was left with him. The street seemed nice, it didn't seem like a rough area, but going into this stranger's house was a gamble.

So, in we go, and to my absolute terror, everything was covered in dust sheets. I suddenly became frozen. I was going to die; he had brought me here to kill me. This room was set up for murder. No one knew I was here except for his friend. Maybe he didn't want me to come here because his mate was a psycho. I soon found myself telling the guy I had to go, and he objected saying I'd freeze out there. I then began pleading for my life, telling him I had young children who needed me. He then became upset. He said he wasn't going to hurt me and he was just trying to help me. He picked up the phone and called his dad. He asked him to explain to me that he was a nice guy and wouldn't hurt me. His dad seemed nice, and I was glad that someone else knew I was here, but I still wasn't completely convinced. I told him I believed him, and he felt confident enough to leave me alone.

While he used the bathroom, I picked up his mobile and texted my lost phone, as it was the only number I could remember. I then found an envelope with an address on it, and sent it over to my phone, with the message 'last place at'. When the guy came back, I told him that I'd sent the message and that everyone would know I was here. He was upset again. He said he would never try and help anyone again, and that he was just a nice guy doing the right thing. We sat uncomfortably for a while. I'd hop out for a cigarette here and there while he was making endless coffee.

After a while, we started chatting, and he was telling me about the work he was having done to the house, hence the dust sheets. I had misjudged this guy. He was just a knight in shining armour. As promised, when morning came, he got me some cash and ordered me a taxi and sent me on my way. I bet he had never been so glad to say goodbye to someone in his life. I had been a nightmare from start to finish. Throughout my hangover, the next day, all I could think of was how that man could have been a murderer, how no one would have known what happened to me and how my kids would have been screwed up for life if I'd have gone missing. I realised that I had a drinking problem, and I needed to sort myself out. Just because my kids didn't see me drunk didn't mean that drink wasn't going to ruin their lives. I had to grow the fuck up.

* * *

The good news was that a kind person had found my phone and they lived near my sister. I would be getting that back at least, but my other stuff had been lost forever. My sister told me that she and Carrie had searched for me but given up and gone home. They even said they'd shouted out for me in the toilets but had heard no reply. It was definitely my fault.

After my scary evening out, the bleak house was just the same, and I was carrying on as usual. My kitchen had been finished, and they were still doing some work on the other one. There was still the hallways to be painted, but we had a beautiful new kitchen. The dining table was the same, and the old worktop fryers were put back in, but it was so much nicer. That was until the smell started.

There was this horrible stench coming from the new drain on the kitchen floor. No one knew what it was at first, but the smell persisted. Then bile started coming up through the drain, flooding the kitchen with shit, so the plumbers had to be called out. The problem lay in a sewage pipe that had been blocked because some tit had been stuffing nappies down the toilet. Given that there was only one young baby left at this time, it was obvious that the culprit was Ashley. Dirty bitch! The stench hung around all day, and we had to go out to eat. I wasn't convinced that she would stop doing it, and it happened a few times over the coming weeks. I couldn't understand why she was here.

Not content with flooding us from the ground up, she went out one day, leaving both of the taps on in the upstairs bathroom, and locked the door using the emergency turn screw on the outside. My kitchen, of course, was directly below it. There was water flooding down the walls into the new units. These kitchens had cost thirty thousand pounds each, and one was now flooded.

A fire engine was called, as it must have been protocol, and as I'm stood at the end of the hallway looking upon the drama, my dishy fireman turns up. My God, the shame! He caught me directly in the eye and smiled at me. I immediately ran back to my room. I had bigged-myself-up to this guy, and here I was, in this refuge, the place where damaged women with an airport load of baggage were sent to slowly wither away. There was no way he would want to speak to me now, not living here. I had not texted him previously, even though I had his number. I had been drunk, he had been drunk, and in the cold light of day, someone like him was never going to like someone like me. Now he had seen where I lived, there was no way I was going to humiliate myself by messaging him. So that was the end of that. Oh, well.

* * *

Rumours were circulating that Ashley was hurting her baby. I didn't like Ashley, but I thought it was a bit mean to say things like that if there was no proof. I did know that the baby had fallen off the bed and had broken a bone in her ankle. But accidents do happen, and Ashley didn't seem all there, so she probably wasn't paying attention. I'm sure this will have scared her enough to be more attentive and not leave her baby on a bed to roll off.

The women were convinced though, given her previous misdemeanours, she was 'cuckoo'. There was a new woman there who had taken Ashley and the baby to the hospital. I hadn't even met this woman yet or known how Ashley got to the hospital. These things happened sometimes, I knew most things that went on, but just sometimes, things eluded me. During the night the new woman had gone to her job as usual, but by the next morning, she had come back and helped Ashley, who was in the next room.

Jen was a teeny, tiny, little Scottish woman with a baby daughter of a few months old. She worked in the day, the baby already had a day nursery, and Jen carried on with her normal life as much as possible. It was very unusual to have someone who kept their job while here, and also someone with a car, that part was strange because it was quite common, with controlling men, that us little women weren't allowed the freedom of a car. I know I hadn't been, and several other women hadn't been.

Jen was breaking the norm here at the bleak house. It was in the evenings that we all got to know her. She became one of us evening wine o'clockers. Jen was open about everything, except how she got to be here. All I knew was that there had been an incident and she had wound up here in the night.

Ashley seemed to want to cling to both Jen and Mary, with them both having young babies. I would often go to Mary's house to find Ashley was just leaving. It seemed that we couldn't be in the same place together, which I found odd. That's how shifty she was. I didn't kiss her arse. I wasn't intimidated by her size, and we had nothing in common. When I went to Mary's, she would make her excuses and leave.

One day, as she was leaving, Mary was seeing her off in the front garden, I rocked up and waited with her. Ashley put the baby in the pram, got five steps away and the pram collapsed, throwing the baby out. Ashley was so upset, but it seemed for herself more than the baby. It took her a moment to even consider picking the baby up. The poor little sweetheart was screaming. Mary called an ambulance while Ashley asked me to check over the baby. There were a few scratches and scrapes, but I was happy knowing she was going to be checked over at the hospital. It was quite the accident.

Upon inspection, it appeared that the pram was missing a locking bolt, which was very odd. I decided there and then that she had tampered with it. If I hadn't heard any rumours previously, then I would have thought it was an accident, that the bolt had come loose due to a manufacturing fault. However, there was no smoke here without fire. I believed that she had deliberately hurt her child, but I couldn't understand how any mother could do that. What happened to this woman's motherly instinct? How crazy was this bitch?

There was talk in the bleak house, and whispers were that she was placed here by social services so they could keep an eye on her. Beryl suggested that she had Munchausen syndrome by proxy. I only remembered this because of the film title Baron Munchausen. I really was finding it impossible to believe that a woman could hurt her child, though. I was battling that idea with the fact that there wasn't proof, but also that this was the second time in weeks that her baby had been to the hospital.

There was a lot of unease amongst us. We didn't want this woman to be left alone with this baby. And what if she hurt our children? On the other hand, we couldn't say anything to her, because we would get into trouble. This was a lose-lose situation for everyone that had to live placidly with this woman.

* * *

Well, I had a nice quiet corridor for some time. That was until Deidre moved in. This woman looked so much older than her thirty-five years. She had three boys under six, and all of them were outrageously hyperactive. Dee just couldn't control them, and they caused mayhem from the moment they arrived. She was quite a small woman with a mousy bob, one of those super easy haircuts for mums who didn't have time to look in the mirror. The way she dressed was simple too, corduroy pants and woolly cardies. Yep, thirty-five going on seventy-five this one was.

Getting to know Dee was fine. She was an easy-going cockney, and she had a faint accent. I didn't blame Dee for her boys being so loud and boisterous. I mean, I didn't think she could cope at all. She didn't know how to discipline them, but maybe they were acting out because of their situation, or maybe they had ADHD, you never know. I did know, however, that these boys were running Dee ragged. They absolutely controlled her.

At bedtime, there was shouting and screaming from the boys and from Dee. I was getting really annoyed with it, my kids had a good bedtime routine, and once I settled them, I went downstairs for a drink and a natter. Now I had this ruckus every night in the room next door. It would usually take around seventy-five minutes to go from screaming to sleeping. It was a relief when they settled down, for everybody, not just Dee.

I was already having trouble wondering how mums could hurt their kids when Elizabeth did something that I couldn't quite believe. She had been slowly becoming friendlier. We didn't ask her for counselling advice as she had already laid the law down on that, and we respected that. Elizabeth was a bit of a part-timer. She went out most evenings. We didn't know where and we didn't ask. She had always dressed well, so it didn't seem odd that she looked nice most evenings. As much as we women thought we were getting to know her, she was still shrouded in mystery and remained that way until she moved out.

I asked her about her new house, as it was unusual for a single lady to get a place so quick. Elizabeth was quite open about the house itself. She had found a house to rent. It was a white cottage in a village, and it was somewhere that no one knew her. It had one bedroom, and I was a little confused as she had two boys. I was under the impression that she was looking for a home for her and her boys, but she wasn't. Elizabeth would shut down if you mentioned the family. I could only assume that they were staying with their father. Not in a million years did any of us expect for them to knock on the door a couple of weeks later looking for their mum. Those poor boys were heartbroken to learn that she had abandoned them. She had set up this love nest for herself and this man she had been seeing. We could only guess that this man was the reason she was out every evening. We even thought that there could have been an affair going on, and that's why she was here. Those two boys didn't deserve to have that evil bitch as their mum. The looks on their faces as they sullied away from the bleak house, not knowing where their mum was or if they would see her again. These things just kept happening in here, and it was disheartening to see kids who were hurt, abused, screamed at or downright neglected. It made me want to cuddle my kids more.

Although I didn't see Vic that much, she still popped over to Mary's, and we would often have a coffee together. That was all about to change, though. Mary was a gossip, and she loved knowing stuff about people. She had no problem sharing her little tidbits, even in the schoolyard. The thing was, Mary didn't care if this stuff was true or not, she shared stuff anyway.

I never really gave anyone a reason to chat shit about me, so I had always remained unscathed from the lipstick mummies. I don't know whether Mary would do this at the school to get people to like her, or just to get their attention, but her tongue was hurting people. I knew she was a gossip, but I was never involved, so I wasn't bothered.

Vic, however, had started hearing things in the schoolyard. Things about a cousin of hers sleeping with a dad at the school. I'd never heard about it, but then I never spoke to any other mums at the school. I only spoke to the bleak house mums. It was different for Vic and Mary. They lived here. This was the place they were settled in. I wasn't staying here, so I had no intention of making mates, to then lose them when I moved like before. Being settled here meant that rumours could cause damage, and Vic was on the warpath.

It hadn't been long since drop off, and I was at Mary's. After putting the kettle on, the door rattled with thuds. Mary answered, and all I could hear from the kitchen was screeching, like a banshee. Vic was exploding, about the rumour that Mary had spread.

I was soon outside in the garden with them both. Vic had her daughter in her arms as she had taken her out of the pram because she was crying. But the two women were still both screaming at each other. Mary was denying all responsibility, asking who had said what and that she hadn't said this and that. Vic was all 'why this?' and 'why that?' It was very repetitive until Mary told the gobby bitch to fuck off! Vic lost it and started punching her in the face. I had remained pretty impartial at this point, but I had to do something. Vic had a baby in her arms. They could scrap until the cows came home, but I was grabbing that baby and getting her to a safe distance, which is what I did. The fight fizzled out after a few punches and some hair-pulling. Mary went into the house while Vic put her hair back in a bun. I pretty much told Vic and Mary that day to not involve me in their spat, which they didn't, but they didn't speak again.

CHAPTER EIGHT

MARCH

I was so used to this place now that I was starting to forget about getting my own house. I had a routine. The kids were settled in the school, even though I didn't like it and the teachers were treating my children differently than the others.

Ellie came home from school crying one day. Her teacher was being mean to her. He shouted at her because she wasn't good at maths. I was very protective of my little sensitive Ellie. I didn't know what had gone on. I just knew that I was livid. It was them versus us, as usual. I went into the classroom the next morning and shouted at him, in front of the class, just to see how he liked it. He didn't. I was seen as one of them 'troubled' mums from over the road, so it was expected of me to be neurotic and erratic. For that reason, the whole thing was brushed under the carpet. I wasn't brought to task for my outburst, and the teacher had been dealt with by me. I left it at that.

I was getting used to having Dee in the next room. Her boys were a nightmare, but they were getting to sleep much more quickly. I didn't think to question why. Not even when Dee asked me to go to the chemist and buy her some Piriton, which I happily did. In fact, over the weeks, Dee asked most of the women to buy her some Piriton. I was not suspicious, I just assumed that it was approaching spring, the kids couldn't sleep because of allergies, and that was that.

The other women were more suspicious than me and realised that Dee was drugging the kids to get them to sleep. No family goes through the copious amounts of antihistamine that they did. She had bought so much of the stuff that the chemists had refused to serve her. Then slowly, the chemists had refused to serve many of us. They were getting used to our faces. I wasn't surprised. However, I did realise that we were all in cahoots with Dee. We didn't do anything to stop her. In fact, we all helped her. It was that pack mentality working at its finest again. Or was it at its worst? We all wanted to get a good night's sleep, and we wanted to be able to settle our children. The only way to do this was for Dee to drug her kids to sleep. It made evenings so much easier, especially for Dee, who was becoming much calmer over time. It got to the point where Dee was getting buses to go to towns further afield just to get the Piriton, and no one batted an eyelid, because we all knew how boisterous and downright monstrous these boys had been previously at bedtimes. I started to see it as a little bit wrong, but I, like others, just turned a blind eye. After all, no one wanted that screaming to return at bedtime.

* * *

I had days in here where I felt like I would have moved into a tent if it meant getting away from this drama. Then oddly, there were some days where it didn't seem that bad. With Dee's boys being so much calmer, and everyone pretty much getting along, it seemed OK.

I finally had some good news. I had a house, and I was ecstatic! A HOUSE! I could have done a jig, whoop whoop! That was until I read the address. Well, it was a house, but there was no way I was going to move into it. I had finally been offered a three-bedroom house, in the town that I had requested, but it was in the absolute worst borough imaginable. I had stated my top three when I applied. There were so many places they could put me, but this place was not happening. I couldn't believe that I would rather stay here than move to this ungodly place. It was like Roughsville, only rougher, and with a worse drug problem. Crime and violence were rife there. The place was notorious for its problems for miles around. There was no way I was moving there.

In my mind, I knew that if I moved there, I would never get out, no-one ever did, and criminals and drug dealers would surround my children. The schools were shocking as well. I couldn't subject my children to that life. I wanted to give them a good start, and that would have ended the dream. I called up the council on the day of the viewing, and I told them I couldn't make it. I told a humdinger of a lie,

"Luke is poorly," I said, "I cannot possibly get two buses with him. It will make him worse." The woman explained that they couldn't hold the viewing and that the next person on the list would view it. I told her that I understood, but Luke's health was my priority. That was that. My house gone. My doing, of course, but still, the hope of having a house had been there, even if fleeting.

The downside now was that I would only have two more house offers. Refusing three houses would get me struck off the waiting list. So I had to pray that the next one wasn't in that area. I was extra hopeful now that after one offer, then next one would surely be on its way pretty swiftly.

It seemed a bit strange to the others that I could refuse a house, especially after how long I had been here, but I was used to it. Not that I was overly choosy. But when I moved, I wanted a nice area for my kids. I couldn't always understand why everyone wouldn't want the same thing. But I did know that it took all sorts to make the world go around, and this place was full of all sorts.

I didn't visit Vic anymore, but I did still spend quite a bit of time with Mary, and with my divorce and her need to spend some time away from the baby, we decided to hit the town. The local club was just a hop, skip and a jump away from Roughsville, no taxi needed. With it being my first night of leaving the kids at Mary's, I wanted to stay close. There was a small part of my brain that thought I was crazy leaving my children in that dump, with a man I barely knew. Then the other part of my brain decided to do it anyway. I had never seen him be mean with his own kids, and I was desperate for a night out. I was putting them to bed first, anyway.

Mary and I had such an amazing night out. The dance music was good, we got along great, and the DJ was fit as hell. He took a shine to me, and he was devoting music to me all night. I felt like the queen of the dancefloor that night. I felt that I looked half decent, and it was probably the best night out I'd had since I'd been here. I didn't much bother with any flirting, and I didn't get so drunk that I had my head in a toilet. I went back to Mary's, climbed into bed with the kids and woke up with my dignity. Something that I had not done for a long time.

My nights out at that club became more regular, and some of the other women wanted in too. Jen and Lynn, who had been quietly squirrelling around the place, seemed keen to come out with me. I didn't mind at all, the more, the merrier. I did decide only to go out when the kids were at their grandparents.

I had been so uneasy leaving them with Mary's fella that one time that I decided not to do it again. I was getting back into going out at least every two weeks. I flirted with the DJ, and I was getting invited to lock-ins. The bouncers got used to my face, and between the three new drinking buddies, I always had someone to go out with. I definitely got more smashed when the kids were at their grandparents because I knew they were safe. With that knowledge, my drinking habits were going downhill again. It seemed like when I drank, I became a different person. I stepped out of my dark and pitiful existence and became confident and carefree. I didn't have any of my issues. I left them at the bleak house.

When I drank, I felt invincible. I felt like I could have any man I wanted and that I was popular. I had no need for petty worries. I had a different character, a persona of the person I wanted to be. Booze did that to me. Of course, I would wake up, and reality would hit. I'd be back in the bleak house with my problems and a hangover. But at least I'd escaped for a few hours, and I couldn't wait to be that character again. I became addicted to wanting to be her, but only the booze would bring her out. I still enjoyed a drink of knock-off vermouth in the evenings, but I shined every other weekend. I began living for it.

Jen and I were getting closer all the time. I had been her saviour on one occasion when she came running to my room in distress. There was a mouse in her baby's cot, and she was terrified. I investigated, but I couldn't find the blighter, it was long gone. But I did go in and brought her baby to her, so she felt like I had saved her. I also think that she was impressed by my fearless attitude toward rodents. It definitely brought us closer together. The woman needed someone to rely on if it ever came back.

Jen did, of course, complain to the staff, and also, out of pure fear for her baby's safety, sent the tot to stay in Scotland for a wee while. She also went to the council to complain. She wanted her house to hurry along, she didn't want to be living with mice, and she wanted her child. It seemed to work, and she got housed pretty quickly after that. She had always promised me though that we would stay friends and have our nights out, and that we did.

I must have really left my mark on people. I was always being invited to stay with people. I was taking them up on it too, anything to get out of this place. I had arranged to go and stay with Sadia. We had a lovely evening. She seemed so different away from the bleak house, less bothered by her life hanging in the balance if she were to be found by Arabian hitmen.

I liked the way she did a lot of things. She was very tidy, but she would not, however, under any circumstances, wash dishes. A house is not a home without a dishwasher. She had the boys do them when we lived together, but I hadn't realised why until now. She was like a little old maid. She was so hospitable, a great cook and good company, but she was slightly old fashioned in her ways. Sadia liked a good old-fashioned bed, with good heavy blankets. She liked her first cuppa of the day to be at a specific time, and in peace. Sadia just liked things a certain way, and I liked the simplicity of it all. What didn't change with Sadia was her nosiness and knowledge of what was going on around her. She was a curtain twitcher, an over-the-fence gossiper, and I found it quite funny, mostly.

The one time it wasn't so amusing was the time that she informed me that Pam's son had been killed in a traffic accident. I didn't know how to feel about it. I believed myself to be a caring person, which is why I was shocked that I didn't seem to care.

I felt that Pam never liked me from the off. I didn't feel like I owed her any compassion now. It was sad that someone had died, but I had stuff of my own to think about. My immediate thought would be that she would be taking time off, and that meant that she would leave me alone, one less thing for me to worry about.

The only things I concerned myself with was getting the kids to school every day, and getting pissed on the weekends, all while waiting for the envelope, or the call to say I had a house.

CHAPTER NINE

APRIL

I always had someone in here that I was close to, as one friend moved out, I became closer to someone else. Lynn and I had been getting closer with each night out. She had a three-year-old boy who would wait for the girls to get home from school so he could play with them. There weren't many young kids in the place anymore. Dee had gone, thankfully, because it could be exhausting turning a blind eye. Ashley was still creeping about, but we all seemed to just ignore her. Nobody wanted to have to live with her, but she seemed to be behaving, for now. There hadn't been an incident for a while.

The room next to me had been empty since Dee left and with no old hag hogging the bathroom anymore, it felt almost like an en-suite. Sunshine was returning to this dark world, and I was getting a little bit of hope back. I mean, honestly, how much longer could I stay in here? My days would be the same. Drop the kids off at school, have a coffee, then either go to someone's house or go shopping, with anyone. It didn't matter who. Get the kids, sort tea, put the kids to bed and drink. I had gotten used to a pattern here now. When it became quiet, that's when I expected the influx of new inmates or residents as the staff called them. Just when I got used to who was around me, a new batch would be thrown into the mix, and by George, a big batch came in.

I was called in to be told the news that I hated to hear, I had to move room. The new family needed two rooms - two flipping rooms! Why would one family need two rooms? I was being moved to the room next to Beryl. It still had two sets of bunk beds, but it was half the size of the room I had now. It was tiny, claustrophobic and with the horrific job of cleaning the kitchen every day. The new family was numerous, nine of them, in fact. One mum had eight kids. Jesus! I would never remember these. So many names, so many faces. There were just kids everywhere. She was like the Pied Piper with kids behind her. Eight kids and she was bloody tiny with no baby weight anywhere. Fair play to her.

The youngest was around two, and the eldest was fifteen. She was very friendly, and she seemed to take a shine to me straightaway. Sandy had told them if they had any questions, to come and ask me, and I didn't mind, as I knew the place as much as the staff. I knew the area very well now too. You'd almost think I was making a life here, but I still had no intention of doing that, no matter what.

I didn't mind that that this family had taken my room. However, I didn't like the upheaval of moving again. I only wanted to move if it was into a house. It was getting increasingly difficult to watch women come and go while languishing in here, not so much for me, but for the girls.

This place was the next level when it came to the quality of living, or lack thereof. I didn't want them to be used to people constantly coming in and out of their lives. I didn't want them to feel a lack of connection like I felt. I certainly didn't want them to think that people were all emotional wrecks with serious issues that affected the way they behaved daily. There was no such thing as normality in this place. No contentment could be found. It was a pit of despair and want with broken women and the odd psycho thrown in just in case anyone was thinking of getting too comfortable.

At least we still had the odd workshop. This month, the theme was based around cooking. I was looking forward to the break in the monotony, something new. The ingredients were all paid for in-house, so free food - ker-ching! The cook who came along was very good. Although the meal was planned the first week, the next time she came we had been given an option on what we would like to cook. We were also given cash and sent away to get the ingredients. Beryl and I volunteered for shopping duty, and we worked well as a team. The time spent cooking was great. I took a real interest, and I enjoyed making the food from scratch, using spices to flavour food instead of relying on a jar or packet. It was great! Then eating together after the meal had been cooked was a bonus. I was easy to get on with anyway, but it was a good bonding experience for many of the other women. I knew that we were going to be doing this for the next few weeks at least, and I had something to look forward to that didn't involve a hangover.

My night-outs were so routine. Sometimes it would be Mary, sometimes, Lynn, sometimes both. I now stayed with Jen on occasion and we became quite close, to the point where she told me how she had come to live in bleak house. Jen had returned home from work one evening to find her boyfriend cheating and in a rage; she had hit him square in the face and broke his jaw. I found this surprising for such a small woman. The police had to remove her from the house they shared, and they brought her to the refuge while telling her not to disclose what had happened, as, by all accounts, she was abusive. The council had no obligation to house her because of the assault, not even in a hotel, so we got her, because she had a young baby. I didn't tell anyone of this, she wasn't there anymore, and I had a great relationship with her.

I knew I still had a drinking problem, but my alter ego had too much freedom to leave behind, I enjoyed being her. So, I continued to have nights out with Mary, and I had permission to stay out until twelve this one particular night. It restricted my style, but I still got to play for a bit.

I had been chatting to a nice young man, a little bit younger than me, and he offered to walk me and Mary home. It was only a four-minute walk, but we could stroll and make it more like ten minutes. Off Mary went to her little haven in Roughsville and off I walked to the side of the bleak house. He didn't realise this was where I lived. I wasn't ready to tell him. It was nothing to do with him and I would never see him again anyway. As I was murmuring that I was heading home, and thanking him for the company, yada-yada, I spotted a group of young men approaching. He asked me to stay where I was. I felt so uneasy, and I asked him if he knew them - he did. They were his friends, and they were indicating that they wanted to have some fun with me. I felt very concerned, scared even, as they were getting closer and laughing with each other. I could make out them saying stuff like, "We'll be having some," and "Who's having it?" I zoned out in a panic, for a few moments like a rabbit caught in the headlights.

Just beyond the bleak house was a field, and I had no intention of going there. It was quite an eerie night too, and it was a little misty. It felt like a scene from a suspense thriller. I sobered up pretty quickly and remembered that Beryl was usually sat by the door smoking around this time of night. I just had to hope that the night staff hadn't locked up yet. I shouted Beryl's name over the wall, and luckily it carried. When she replied, it was like music to my ears. I shouted over.

"Are those security cameras pointing this way?"

"Aye."

The men started backing away.

"Yeah, you fucking arseholes! Off you fucking go!"

I shook for hours. I'd done it again. I'd got into a situation where I could have got raped and murdered. Why did this keep happening to me? I definitely needed to change my strategy, my super confident alter ego kept landing me in vulnerable situations, and the only thing I cared for more than me right now was the kids getting a nice home and a decent upbringing. Not very easy with a mum who kept getting into dangerous situations like these.

Why were men such wankers anyway? I was losing hope that there were any decent blokes out there. My biggest problem was that I was too friendly when I was on the drink. I saw everyone as my friend, men, and women alike. It's just that more men happened to chat with me, and there was an obvious reason. But I never promised them anything. They just assumed that if I spoke back to them that they were getting lucky. Idiots!

* * *

The time had come; I had finally got an appointment for counselling, and luckily it was very close. There was also availability when Luke was in playgroup. I never knew what to expect, but I was a talker, so I was interested to see what would happen. The counsellor was a very slender, pretty lady with a lot of blond curly hair put into a messy bun on the top of her head. I noticed her vivid blue eyes and coral lipstick. I don't know why I paid so much attention. Maybe it was to make a judgement on whether to trust her with my emotional shit.

She explained that it was a safe space to share and that our chat was confidential. I didn't seem to have a problem chatting. In fact, I had to reign it in. I was pretty much trying to get my entire life story out in one hit. But she garnered some control over the conversation and picked out bits that we used as a focus. A more purposeful conversation ensued, and I was talking about things that I thought I'd long forgotten. I sometimes felt I was whinging, and I didn't like that as I wasn't a moaner. I didn't like it all being about me, me, me. The woman had to remind me that this hour was to focus on me, so that's what we did.

The first thing I spoke about was why I was living in the refuge and why I felt the need to move away. With a simplistic view, I knew I had to escape an abusive partner, but I soon realised that it was to go deeper than that. I found I was talking about a time before I even met *that man* and my relationships with men in general. I didn't have any daddy issues, that was made clear. I was actually a daddy's girl, I adored my father, and we always had a close bond. I am the baby of the family with two brothers and a sister. I was a loved child, so my man issues didn't stem from there. There was one thing that happened that could've been to blame, and I blurted it out. Even though I didn't think I'd be believed and even though I hadn't mentioned it since it happened, yet here it was.

I remembered that when I was around eight years old, I had been playing with a group of boys, my brothers' friends. We were all playing in a small area along the riverbank, where there were little dens, some green areas with bushes and trees, and stone walls hiding the area from the nearby houses. I noticed that my brothers had gone somewhere, leaving me with a much older boy. I'd say he was around thirteen, but I wasn't sure. He suddenly grabbed my hand and shoved it into his pants and made me keep it there. In turn, he put his hand in my knickers. I was completely devoid of any emotion. I can just remember thinking this is wrong. I didn't know what to think, or what to do, I just knew that it made me feel really bad and I had to try and get away from there. He said that he wanted me to take off my knickers, and I then became more fearful. I said that I needed to wee and that I would just go behind the bush to do so. I went behind the bush, and ran for safety, up the embankment and to the road.

I felt sick and worried. I wondered what I had done to make him do that to me. I realised from this session that those feelings had never gone away. I felt that I was giving something off that made men think they could treat me that way, and just take from me. I had my innocence taken from me that day. I told a friend, an older girl who had been part of the group, but she told me to stop making things up. I realised then that no one would believe me, so I didn't mention it again, until now.

There was still no emotion, just shock. I still had to question myself on whether I had led that boy on. Had I asked for it in some way? It was a question that I had in my subconscious for so long that a simple 'it wasn't your fault' just didn't suffice as an answer. It became clear that this event had probably shaped my whole perception of what relationships should be like. That men can just treat me like crap, and it's probably me giving something off which attracts them. Fuck! What an eye-opener. I had to stay single forever. It certainly did explain a lot. I'd endured ten years of a relationship where I was emotionally manipulated, intimidated, and abused psychologically, financially, socially, as well as occasionally sexually and physically. Yet I didn't tell anybody, I feared I wouldn't be believed. That man was so charming in front of everyone else that there was no way that anyone would believe a bad word against him.

This was proven when we separated. I had friends accusing me of lying, which I couldn't understand, as I'd never been prone to fantasy. So why would I lie? I went to the police to tell them I was scared. They wouldn't help unless they caught him in the act. They told me to call them when he attacked me, which I couldn't do as he kept confiscating my phone. Then my solicitor spoke to me like I was delusional. I began to feel paranoid, and it made me almost reclusive like I really had to fight this man on my own.

I went to Women's Aid as a last resort, and they explained areas that I hadn't even realised were abuse. Another friend I spoke and said I was fine until I went to the Women's Aid. She said that they had filled my head with all sorts. I was getting more and more paranoid believing he was kerb-crawling in his works van, or he'd have the nose of the van peeking out around corners. I was getting too afraid to leave the house, but yet, no one believed me. Story of my life, I had newly discovered.

I genuinely couldn't understand what it was about him that had everyone thinking he was angelic, and what it was about me that made people think I would suddenly turn on my husband and start making things up. I couldn't fathom it. But this was all coming out in the counselling, questions surrounding my fear of telling people things in case I'm not believed. To be honest, I didn't even think the counsellor believed me. I had been conditioned to feel that no one would ever believe me. That any tale I told was a fabrication. This was certainly not what I was expecting during this counselling session. I thought the first one would be easy. I had so much more that I wanted to say. I had things in my mind that I had never spoken about to anyone, and I felt like I wanted to offload now, while I was sharing, but then at the same time I didn't, because saying stuff makes it real. I realised that our time had come to an end. It went so quickly. We made plans to meet again in a couple of weeks.

I was unsure of how I felt about counselling. I knew my mind was processing lots of stuff, emotions were bubbling to the surface, and I started to feel something, which was so odd as I hadn't felt anything remotely emotional for months. But it was there, yes, upset. Damn it! I felt upset. This couldn't be happening, and if I let my emotions come out, I would be seen as weak and out of control. My strategy was to stay completely in control of my feelings, so I didn't lose it and have a breakdown and lose the kids. I wasn't sure if I should do counselling if it was going to do this to me.

* * *

It took days for me to feel more in control after the counselling. The processing bit really did control me for a while there, and I stayed out of people's way for a bit. But when I was ready to come back into the thick of the bleak house life, I soon realised that there was an old face in the kitchen. Fucking Tracey! What was that bitch doing back here? I thought she was meant to be starting a new life in Cornwall.

Janet had discovered that she was a lying conniving cow-bag. She didn't have breast cancer at all. She had made it up for the attention. How did she have the audacity to come back here?

They must have told her that I was still here as she didn't seem surprised. I hated this woman with a passion. But as usual, I had to grin and bear it, and she knew that. There she was being nice to everyone like butter wouldn't melt, but I knew better. I decided to bite my lip and not tell anyone what this abomination of a person was really like. I decided that I would stay well away from her, she wasn't in my kitchen anyway, so it would be easy. There were times when we would have to be around each other, like workshops, but I could easily ignore her.

I was still enjoying the cooking classes, and I really did like the cook too. She was very good at what she did and led this group well. What I didn't like about the class was Beryl. Or moreover, what she decided to do, in front of me. She was stealing utensils. Oh, dear God, why do that in front of me? I really liked this cook, and those are her things. I agonised about what to do. I felt torn as I got along so well with Beryl, but what she did was putting the workshops at risk, and no doubt upsetting the cook.

I didn't know if it was the once or if she had done it before. I was in a quandary now. I can't believe she put me in this position. I felt like I had no option. I had to go to the office. I didn't mention Beryl's name, but I did report that someone had been stealing utensils from the cook. I just had to. It wasn't fair. I left it at that and waited for the fallout and along it came.

They must've known it was her, and she must've known it was me who ratted her out because she stopped speaking to me. In fact, she outright turned her nose up at me. I would get eye rolls every time I went into the kitchen. She would make a show of offering everyone a drink except me, and she would mumble under her breath. It was extremely childish, and I was starting to feel like I couldn't go in the kitchen anymore. But I also just wanted to ignore her and go about my business.

Slowly, many other women began ignoring me too. It was the pack mentality coming out again, this time against me. Ah well, all those sheep were welcome to her. I had Lynn still, who didn't get involved with the pack. Everyone else pretty much followed her example and stayed away from me.

I noticed that new women wouldn't approach me either, as she was getting there first, and giving them a friendly heads up to stay away from me. I don't know what she was saying, and I didn't care. A lot of these women would come and go briefly anyway.

One evening she made dinner for the whole of the bleak house. The staff knew about it, and the other women were in on it. I didn't find out about it until it was happening. When I walked in the kitchen to make tea, there they all were like a cackle of witches, enjoying their slap-up meal without me. She really did have a vendetta, but I chose to stay away from her.

Not all the newbies wanted to be in Beryl's gang. Some had more sense than to listen to shit about people as soon as they walked through the door. I didn't realise it at the time, but I had a secret ally.

Jude was a no-nonsense kind of woman. She was definitely different from the usual guest here at the anti-haven. This woman seemed strong-minded, not the type to take crap, fair and open, and she was a breath of fresh air. I was surprised to learn that she was a bouncer, the sort who could take care of herself. So why was she in here? That is something I never found out, as she wasn't one to talk about herself. But she certainly did command respect, and she didn't suffer fools.

Jude was a large lady. She was overweight but carried it well, and it added to the whole bouncer image. She had blonde, curly but amazingly thick, uncontrollable hair. I discovered that she also worked at some stables, a job that she was trying to maintain.

The first time that I realised that Jude wanted to help me out was when she introduced herself. She had been watching the goings-on with Beryl and also paid attention to me. She decided that I wasn't the bitch that Beryl wanted people to believe. Jude told me that Beryl had told her straight away to stay away from me because I was a trouble-maker. However, all Jude had seen was her being nasty towards me, so Jude made her own mind up.

As per my room, it was my daily chore to clean that kitchen. I would prefer to do it in the late afternoon, that way people would be tidier generally after dinner. So, as usual, I cleaned the kitchen until it was spotless, I always did a thorough job. I had to get Linda to tick off the job in her book, so off I went to locate her and bring her back.

As I entered the kitchen, Jude was pushing a microwave back into place, and I thought it was a bit odd. Linda came in to inspect the kitchen, and Beryl, bold as brass, walked over to the microwave, pushed it aside and said I wasn't cleaning properly. The look on her face when she realised the area was spotless, was priceless. I realised what had happened. Jude knew she had planted dirt under the microwave to get me in trouble, and she had quickly removed it before Beryl saw her. Brilliant! An ally indeed. I felt a deep sense of satisfaction, ha fucking ha Beryl! You dick!

Beryl seemed to leave me alone for a while. So did the other women. But I didn't have time for playground shit. I just stayed out most days and watched films with the kids before they went to bed. I did have Lynn and Jude and my nights out. I was doing fine for now.

CHAPTER TEN

MAY

Beryl may have pottered around the kitchen constantly, but I had to try and not let her stop me from going in there. I still enjoyed a small tipple of an evening, and it was still my kitchen. Ashley was still hanging around. She would just leave the baby in the pram in the corridor, that was commonplace. Jude was usually in there anyway, like my little guardian angel, making me feel better.

She took me to one side one evening. She wanted some information on Tracey. She asked me if she had told people that she'd had breast cancer. Ooooh, I didn't want to get involved in whatever this was, but I was also not going to lie for that heifer. I told her, yes, but it was none of my business. Jude surprisingly thanked me for not gossiping about it. Jude made it clear that she respected that, not because she liked Tracey. In fact, it was the opposite.

Tracey had been dating Jude's cousin and spreading lots of shit around about him, stuff that wasn't true. Jude respected my dignity, she felt she could trust me, and it was refreshing to hear. We had mutual respect for one another. Jude began to open up more, and I found out so much more about her, she was fascinating.

The best thing I discovered was that she was a white witch. I couldn't believe it, a real white witch, in the bleak house. I was in awe. Jude was happy to share little spells and incantations. I learned so much from her. This was the start of an exciting journey into the surreal.

The first thing that Jude taught me, and several others, was to use fire for cleansing our minds. It was great, like a mini class for healing our hatred of men. She gave us all paper and made us write the men's names on them. We had to write that we were free from them, and we were now empowered. We then had to burn them and let the ashes go up to the cosmos. It was bizarre, but I enjoyed doing it. Of course, someone spoilt it by reporting Jude to the office, for using witchcraft. I don't know what happened in the office, but witchcraft in the open stopped and just a select few of us became privy to Jude's private little group, we would meet in our rooms and carry on learning spells for empowerment and procurement.

* * *

My counselling session soon came around, and I wondered whether I should go. I felt like I should give it a fair chance. I was still feeling shame from the last revelation, and I knew it could get worse before it got better. But I already felt like I was going to hell in my mind, so what did I have to lose? My marbles were already gone.

We seemed to carry on with my view of relationships. It was obviously tarnished heavily. I didn't hate men. I just couldn't understand how I had managed to get such a horrible one. I didn't think I deserved it. Maybe I did, I wasn't sure. Just as in the previous session, the focus moved onto other relationships leading up to this one.

Just prior to my meeting *that man,* I had been dating someone much older than me. I had just turned sixteen, and he was twenty-six. He was a workman that had been working on my friend's house. Their renovations took a while, and I spent a lot of time there, flirting with him. He was attracted to me too. I liked the idea of someone a bit older. It was cool at my age, and he wasn't bad looking either.

We began spending time together. He would pick me up in his Capri, and we would drive around, stop off at the odd pub and have a drink. My age was never questioned. We would kiss a lot in the car, but I wouldn't have sex with him. Maybe it was lack of opportunity, but the moment never seemed to come around. It fizzled out once the work was finished on my friend's house anyway.

One evening, I went out with two friends. We went to a town not too far away and ended up in a new little wine bar. To my surprise, the workman was in there. He lived in the flat above and after closing he invited the three of us up there where we carried on drinking. He was flirting with me a lot, but I wasn't having any of it. I just wanted booze and music, or I did until I felt sick. I was a small person with copious amounts of alcohol in my system. I stayed in the bathroom for quite a while. I began to hear a ruckus of sorts, and my friend wasn't happy about something. I came out of the bathroom, and she was yelling at me.

"You know he has a girlfriend, and a kid, don't you?"

Well, I didn't, but I was trying to explain to her that I wasn't doing anything with him. But she kept banging on, and my head couldn't take it. It was her screaming at me to stay away from him, me screaming that I wasn't doing anything and the next thing we were catfighting. I didn't know what the hell was going on.

My friend wanted to leave, and we were meant to be sleeping at her friend's. But she wouldn't take us both in case we started scrapping again, so they left me there. I was upset and accepted several drinks off the workman, who was still trying his luck. I told him it was not happening, and I was concerned about how easily he forgot about his girlfriend and child. I mean, I hadn't seen it previously, but there was a picture of them on his sideboard. She obviously didn't live there. This was a proper man's flat, everything was black, so I didn't know what the deal was, but I wasn't that girl. I just needed to sleep, so I drifted off on the sofa.

What happened through the night remains a mystery. It wasn't so much that I drifted off, more like I passed out. I woke in the night to feel a lot of weight on top of me, and heavy breathing, then I passed out again. I then woke up in his bed. I was really confused. I didn't know what had happened. Had I had sex? I never consented to any sex. But did I have sex? I was having flashbacks of the brief moment of alertness, him on top of me, breathing heavily and grunting slightly. I started to feel sick. I needed to get away from there. I had to sneak out.

I found a phone box and got my brother to come and get me. I was dizzy trying to figure out what had happened. I couldn't tell anybody anything because I didn't understand anything, and as for my friend, well, I couldn't tell her what I thought might have happened because of our scrap. None-the-less, I felt that I put myself in that position by drinking too much. I blamed myself and tried to forget about it. I couldn't prove anything, and I couldn't tell anyone. I thought I'd add it to my list of secrets. I met that man shortly after, and the rest, as they say, is history.

Counselling was certainly insightful. No wonder I didn't like men anymore. Saying these things out loud made them very real, and for the first time since it happened, I'd questioned if I had been raped. It was too confusing to even think about before, but I thought I might as well get it out, talk about it, process it, so it wasn't a dirty, shameful secret anymore. I had to accept that this wasn't my fault, just like the assault when I was eight. I didn't ask for it or do anything to make them think that they could do that to me. However, I always hated the word victim, and I refused to be one, even though the effects of these events were clearly causing me a head fuck.

I'd had too much. I was in my twenties, and I'd had more than I could handle. I wasn't strong enough to deal with these revelations. It had to come out, but it sure felt like a Pandora's box. I wish I'd have left it be. I explained to my counsellor, I had no right to moan and whinge, as some people live through systematic abuse from their families. Some people endured years of beatings. There were prisoners of war, and people in third world countries who couldn't eat and also had high infant mortality rates. I didn't feel like I had a right to feel sorry for myself.

That was something that my counsellor wanted us to discuss. She wanted to talk about why I felt that my issues were less valid than other peoples. I really couldn't understand why, and we had to leave it for that week. But still, no amount of talking was going to make me feel that I had more right to moan than someone who had bad luck their whole lives. I didn't think I had the right to believe I had it that bad. Those thoughts confused me. Maybe it would become more apparent with the mental processing that I now knew would happen for the next few days.

* * *

Days were turning into weeks here. I had been at the bleak house for nine months, three times longer than the average wait for a house. The kids had almost finished a whole academic year at that shitty school. I did enjoy picking them up, and if it weren't for the children, I wouldn't have anything to live for. My goal was to nurture them and to protect them.

Teatime was usually a bit crazy around the kitchen. I was busy one evening making the kids tea when I heard a bit of shouting in the hallway. It was from Ashley. She had shouted at one of the kids, my kid to be exact. Jude came in and told me that Ellie was playing with a ball, and it had hit the pram in the corridor. Ashley had told her that if she bounced the ball again, then she would bounce Ellie around the walls.

Jude got Ashley to come in the kitchen and goaded her to deny it. Ashley couldn't. I was livid! I squared up to the evil bitch.

"If you ever threaten my daughter again, or even look at her the wrong way I will bounce you around this fucking kitchen! You fucking got me?"

Ashley nodded sheepishly. I was fuming that an adult could threaten a six-year-old. No one threatens my kids, but now I had to worry about getting kicked out for being intimidating to another resident. I waited and waited for the call from the office, but surprisingly it never came. I think Ashley knew that complaining about me would have got her thrown out as well for threatening a child, so it wouldn't have been in her best interest.

I was getting really worried about Ellie. She was drifting into a quiet phase, and she was not handling this environment well. Her happy nature was getting lost in it all, and she wasn't herself. Whereas Nicole just got on with everything, took it all in her stride and never became perplexed at all. Ellie, however, was just becoming more and more unhappy as the days wore on.

This threat knocked her for six, and she couldn't take it anymore. She started begging me to let her stay with her aunty. I told her to wait for the half-term, but she didn't want to. She wanted to leave and not come back. Once she had the idea in her head, it was fixed there, and she would cry every night, begging me to let her go.

I was getting so upset but started to think if my precious girl didn't feel safe, I may have to let her go. I spoke to my sister, and she agreed to let her stay there for a while. I then spoke to the staff in the office, and they explained how it would work. I had a three-month window where Ellie could stay with a relative. After three months, social services would have to step in and determine what would be suitable. So if she had to stay any longer, would that be a feasible and suitable home for her? There was no way in hell that I wanted social services involved. So I had to make sure I was out of there in three months, that was my deadline.

I agreed to let Ellie go, and it broke my heart. But it was the only choice I had. Just to get one of the kids out of the bleak house was a blessing in disguise. Ellie got on so well with her cousins, and I knew she would be so much happier there.

I took her there and stayed the first night with her, I had to make a lot of calls, but I got her into the local school. Then all I could do after that was phone her regularly and visit as much as I could. I missed her beautiful smile. I knew it wouldn't be for long, but my heart was breaking. I was only consoled by the fact that she sounded so much brighter when I called her. Her sparkle was returning, and even though she was missing me, she was in the right place at the right time for her.

I needed a house more than ever now, and I was in Jude's little coven, so I set about asking for her guidance. Jude suggested a bit of candle magic. I had to get a green candle for attraction, and I had to carve into the candle images of what I wanted to receive. I carved little houses, and some money signs so I could get money for furniture. The rest was simple. I had to believe that I would get it and then burn the candle down.

We weren't allowed candles in our room, so I did this under cover of darkness. I burned it for twenty minutes each night before I went to bed, believing each night that I was creating my destiny. Jude said it was cosmic ordering, a bit of a new thing, but the results were supposed to be amazing. I was willing to try anything as I had been here so long, I was now resorting to magic.

I loved listening to Jude talk about her beliefs. Being a white witch meant that she would never use magic to harm anyone. It was only used for good and positive outcomes. There were lots of things that fascinated me, like the use of herbs for illness, crystals for energy works, and colours for wellbeing. It was something I was interested in. I had always loved crystals but had never really learned about them. I found a spiritual shop in the town centre and went in. I spent time with the crystals, seeing which one I was drawn to. I bought my first one, a lapis lazuli, a beautiful blue and grey crystal with little gold flecks. I was mesmerised and kept it with me always. I used this stone to focus on magical stuff. Jude had me meditating and goal-setting and doing all sorts of things that helped me feel more positive. Our little coven would use a pack of playing cards as make-shift tarot cards and we would read our fortunes, mine was always hopeful.

We still had to keep it all a secret. Jude didn't want to get thrown out because people were afraid of her beliefs. Every night I would light that candle and believe, then every morning I would hide it in case we had a room spot check.

My new interest in the spiritual was keeping me occupied, but I wasn't becoming as positive as I would have liked because I was missing my little princess. With the counselling and Ellie's absence, I sometimes feared I was getting worse. It didn't help that Beryl was still causing me problems. She was doing the same thing as she had done to women before me, such as moving my things, making me feel like I was going crazy. She was probably dunking my coffee cup in the toilet, I would not put it past her, as I'd seen her do it to others. I hated that she was in the room next to me, but luckily, she wasn't making noises to disturb the kids. She liked a good lie-in, so I think she knew it was in her best interest not to wake my kids in the night because I would have certainly woke her up early in the morning.

I never watched TV anymore. There wasn't much opportunity. There were no aerials in the rooms, and there was one tiny rubbish telly in the lounge, and it wasn't worth sitting in there as the sofas did not feel clean.

The end of the month, however, was a different story. Big Brother, season five was on, and I'd been waiting all year for this. It was one of the most popular shows on T.V. and worth sitting in that dank lounge for. I watched them go in, and it was great. My excitement was building for the second night.

However, it was not to be. Beryl realised that I was planning on watching it every night, so she got in there first with a blanket and a brew to watch something else. The T.V. was on a first-come, first-serve basis. Once she was in there, I couldn't turn it over until she had finished with it. What a fucking bitch! She also had some of her pack in there with her, watching whatever she chose to put on, anything, as long as it wasn't Big Brother. She really was petty.

I began to think that she wasn't having issues with her daughter, and it was probably her daughter who was bullied by her. Either that or she was abusing the system for a house. I did not believe that she was ever a victim of abuse.

CHAPTER ELEVEN
JUNE

The beginning of this month was exciting for me. It was the end of the half-term, and Ellie was coming back for a couple of days to go on a trip that the staff had organised for us. We were all going to a theme park, and when I say all, I mean just the mums with kids. No Beryl, yay! Ashley was going, unfortunately. I'm not sure why, as the baby wasn't able to go on any rides. But she was a mum, and she had to be included. Old Mother Hubbard was there with her massive brood, and they took up most of the bus, but it was nice to see them have some fun.

As per the British weather, it was drizzly all day. This forced me into the soft play barn, which I didn't mind, as I had Luke anyway. So, no rides for me. I stayed there for a while, a few of us did, including

Ashley, until eventually some of the kids got bored and wanted to move on.

I quickly realised that one of Nicole's shoes was missing. Everyone searched high and low for it. I had learned to be suspicious around some of these women, and I was pretty sure that Ashley had taken it. I looked in bins, toilets, bushes, all sorts of places and it was nowhere to be found. Ashley denied seeing it, but I just knew she had taken it. My poor little girl had to walk through puddles, on hard concrete, on wet grass, all without a shoe, because of that evil cow. I'd really had enough. That candle magic needed to start working faster.

I was so unhappy to see Ellie leave again, but she really was more content staying with my sister. I think that Nicole missed her too, even though she just ploughed on, it must have been hard for her.

I was still having my nights out. Lynn was still here, though not for long as she had a house, a little further afield than most of the women who had been through here. It was a shame, but again, she gave me an open invitation to go and stay with her anytime.

We still had a night out to go before she left. My kids were again at their grandparents, and to save a curfew, I had arranged to stay at Mary's. I didn't get there, though. After a lock-in at the club, my hot DJ invited me back to his place. I had the ladies blessing as they had watched us flirting for a couple of months and knew we were going to get it on at some point.

I didn't feel worried about going anywhere with him. Mainly I think because there were witnesses, and also because I felt good vibes from him. When we left the club, I found out that he had a hot car as well, a nice little sporty number. He also had a nice house. There was no way he was just a DJ.

We had a great night, and for once I didn't talk for hours. I wanted to get straight to the fun stuff, and he didn't disappoint. I needed this experience. I was only in my twenties, and it had been a while. We did all the chatting the next morning, and I told him all about me, the kids, my situation, the lot. That may have been too much too soon, as I didn't hear from him after that. I would have to wait now until I saw him in the club again, to ask him what game he was playing.

* * *

My counselling was still going on. We were still getting to the meaty parts, such as why I was walked all over by a controlling good-for-nothing idiot. I was more concerned with why I was still being controlled even after we split up. I felt that more emotional damage was done after I had the strength to throw him out. Apart from letting the kids down, he was still very much finding ways to abuse me, and one type of abuse was worse than all of the others, the sexual abuse.

I really don't know how he did it. But after being separated for a few months, he ended up back in my bed. I think it was by using emotional blackmail or making me feel sorry for him, or maybe he told me for the umpteenth time that he was going to commit suicide that made me do it. I can never recall how it came to be. I think he was grinding me down so much that it was easier to sleep with him. Maybe he was winning the battle of manipulation, and I was thinking of taking him back. For whatever reason, we were sleeping together.

But it wasn't just me he was sleeping with, he was also having sex with his girlfriend, the woman that he had now married—the woman he was using to flaunt in my face. I didn't have a problem with her per se, she was just being used to get at me. I almost felt sorry for her. But the issue I had was that he was sleeping with her, then coming to me and doing the same thing. I don't know why I had let myself be disrespected in this way; it was definitely a pattern for me. As far as I was concerned, we weren't together, so he wasn't cheating on me, he was cheating on her.

The sexual encounters only happened a few times, and each time he would tell me that his girlfriend had done this and that so much better than me. He would say that she was prettier, thinner, and sexier. Oh, she was the bee's knees and a sex goddess. Every sexual thing I did, she was better at. I got the whole lot.

"Thank god I found her., She makes me happy. She is so much better than you. I don't know what I saw in you. No one will ever want a mess like you."

He was literally comparing me to his girlfriend while his dick was still hard and making me feel worthless in the meantime and yet still wanting to come back to me for sex. I stopped all that. I'd finally had enough.

He must have realised that he had pushed me too far. He asked me for one more opportunity to talk to me, and I agreed. I arranged for my brother to watch the kids and we went for a drive. He drove, and he drove, miles away, and he was fast running out of petrol. He said he didn't have money for more. I told him I just wanted to go home. He wasn't talking, and he was freaking me out. He parked up, and put a song on, Daniel Bedingfield's 'If You're Not the One'. He played it over and over and over again. He held my hand tightly in his while he sang to me. This was not romantic; it was scary as hell. I was terrified, and he refused to take me home, saying he had no petrol again.

We were sat there half the night with that bloody song ringing in my ears. I refused to look at him. I just stared out of the window and stayed there until he snapped out of this thing he was doing. The only words from me were requests to go home. Eventually, he went to a petrol station and filled the car up. It had been a lie about not being able to get home.

On the way back he pulled onto a bridge, informing me that this is where he was going to kill himself. He said he was just going to disappear one day soon, and he would come here to end it, and that it would be my fault. I didn't even feel guilty for wanting him to hurry up and do it already. He eventually dropped me home. I felt thankful to be back, as it nearly time for the kids to get up.

Over the next couple of weeks, he threatened suicide a lot. So much so, that I called his dad and told him to sort him out. He was furious that I did that. I was breaking his rules about keeping it within my walls. He didn't ever think I would contact his family. That was a lesson for him, but it didn't keep him away, though. That's why after a year since the split he was still harassing me to the point of me having to move.

* * *

There was definitely a pattern forming around the way men were using me sexually. My D.J. had been the sneakiest one by far. He worked on the flirting to get me in the sack. He had a good game. I saw him not long after. I managed to get out the next weekend because I needed to see him. He was smiling at me all night, maybe he wanted part two, or maybe he was nervous, I'm not sure.

The bouncers invited me for a lock-in, I knew they would. I made a beeline straight for music boy. I asked him straight out what was going on, and his honesty was refreshing, even if it was disappointing. He said he didn't want to be in a relationship with a woman who had kids. Fair enough, but I couldn't leave it there. I told him that life was always better with kids in it, and it was his loss for feeling that way. But we parted on good terms. I still went there drinking, and if any man came flirting, he would always be watching, a bit conflicting of him, but flattering too. I did turn down lock-ins after that.

I had been in a dark place, mentally since I arrived here. At times I thought I could not get any lower. I had scraped the gateway to Hell, and I knew there was no way it could get worse, but it started to feel like it now.

I was so used to feeling numb that I started to think that's who I was. I certainly put on a good act. I had to, for the kids, but I felt like I was starting to lose it now. With Ellie living away from me, Beryl bullying me, my

DJ out of the picture and my bubbly bunny Lynn leaving, I really was starting to feel this deep despair. Each night I would get worse. I had my little candle ritual I did each night, and I'd feel a little high for a while after that. Then I would try to sleep.

Most nights, I used a little meditation that Jude had advised, but my mind struggled to keep focus. There was too much darkness in there. I started to feel oppressed. I began to get these strange feelings that I was being watched. I was panicking that one of these spells had unleashed something, but it was only white magic, so it was highly unlikely. I had crystals to protect me, and I was fine. Still, each night I was going to bed and feeling this heavy darkness. Not like the darkness from it being night-time, it was darker than that, a hollow black, just nothingness, and it was starting to freak me out. I thought I was going mad. I could feel something in the corner of the room, every night, just waiting and watching. This was definitely madness now, and I couldn't tell anyone, I'd be bloody committed. All I could do was hug Luke and hope it would go away. It didn't though. It just stayed there. I seemed to get used to it, I was still terrified by it, but I was used to it, night after night, just watching me. This was my lowest point. I had to do something and soon. The kids had been keeping me going, any strength I had to fight this darkness was because of them, but time was running out to get Ellie back, and I needed a miracle.

I was spending my time between meeting with my various friends that I had made here: Mary, Lynn, Jen, Sadia, and occasionally Vic. I was also messaging my old friends and my family. I called Ellie a lot, especially on her birthday, which was on a weekday, so I didn't see her. I did manage to make her sports day at school though, I surprised her, and her face looked like it was Christmas day. It was that look that was telling me I had to find a house myself. I could not wait for a council house any longer. I didn't have a clue where to start, and if I had, I would have done this months ago. I had no money for a deposit. I literally needed that miracle I had asked for, but this time for a private rental.

Even though I was keeping busy, and daydreaming about the house we might get, and even getting clued up on all things spiritual, anything that would help get out of here faster, I was still shrouded in darkness. That thing was getting bigger and stronger, and although I was used to it, going to bed was getting scary, something had to give. I was going cray-cray. I was even getting scared of my own shadow.

Then one night, something terrifying and magical happened, I felt the presence, but it had morphed from just a thing in the corner to an actual demon waiting to leap onto me, like literally take my soul. It was going to jump into me and possess me. Then I would be under its influence forever. There would be no turning back. I honestly wasn't sure if I had any fight left in me. I think I felt like I had to succumb to it. This was it. This was the end of life as I knew it. The darkness was about to take me, and I was powerless to stop it. It leapt, and then the magic occurred. A giant golden lion jumped onto me instead. I didn't see it with my eyes as they were closed, but I knew it was there. I could sense this golden light through my eyelids. The lion was some sort of being from the hierarchy of angels. It made it clear to the demon that it wasn't having me, that I was too good, and I had work to do. I didn't know what, but something. I felt so peaceful that I fell asleep straight away

I woke up the next morning, and all of the darkness had lifted. I felt no oppression, I felt light, like I could walk on air, and I felt happy. It was a very strange feeling, indeed. I felt like I should whistle or hum or sing. My whole world seemed brighter, and it was magical. Everything that occurred over that day was brilliant. Not because anything special happened - apart from fighting my demons and winning.

I went out, and the sky was bluer, the grass was greener, and the flowers were so colourful. I just had this feeling going around in my head that I was needed. I had work to do, and I had been saved. I felt like a spiritual change had occurred. Demons didn't possess me, but I had a light instilled in me instead. Nothing could annoy me now, not even Beryl. I set to creating a new spell. I got a new green candle, engraved it, drew a picture of a house on a piece of paper, and I was really specific. I mean, why not?

I asked for a house with a modern fitted kitchen, a bath, a shower, a garage, leather sofas, and in one of three specific areas where I wanted to live. I put the drawing under the candle and spent the next couple of weeks burning it down. I was reading books, buying good luck charms and amulets, and built a stunning collection of crystals. I began mentally preparing for a move. I knew it was coming. I could feel it in my bones.

I loved this new me. I was bouncier, brighter, more content, and I didn't feel crazy anymore. So maybe it wasn't a coincidence that my counsellor called to say that she had been relocated and couldn't see me anymore. There was a little pang in me, a feeling that said, whoa, my shit scared her away. I can't believe she abandoned me, but then I decided that there was no point dwelling on something that I couldn't change. She was there when I most needed her, and maybe now I didn't. That was a good thing. I still needed to work on my self-esteem, but I was definitely feeling more confident just from the epic otherworldly battle I'd already fought in the still of the night.

CHAPTER TWELVE

JULY/AUGUST

I had to get a shift on with this house now. There was only six to seven weeks left to get my princess back, and the clock was ticking. I knew there were just a few weeks of term to go, and then I would be allowed some time away to go house hunting.

I cleared it with my parents that I could go there and use their house as a base, but it would all have to be quick when it happened. I would have to find funding for a deposit, and I would have to apply for a furniture grant.

After living here for nearly a year, I had learned a few tricks from people who had left before me. There were ways of maximising grant pay-outs, and it was all about the children's stress. The more emphasis I put on the children's quality of life, the more money that you could get. I had already started preparing my statement for when I 'got out'. The money would be awarded if your child was so stressed that they had nightmares and were bed-wetting. You could get money for carpets, white goods, and beds, all of the big stuff. There were decorating grants available too. It was all about knowing where the sources of funding were and what to say.

I wanted these next few weeks to go as quickly as possible. As much as I had confidence in finding somewhere to live, I also needed this place as a safety net if I failed. I couldn't just leave. There was still the rule that if you had somewhere to stay, then you didn't need a room here, and I definitely needed that room.

For a start, all of my stuff was still in there: my pots, pans, cutlery, towels, and all manner of houseware. I'd already lost stuff, and I didn't want to have to give it away again. I knew once the holidays came, they would allow me some time out. But for now, I had to stay put. There were already new people moving in, but I had no interest in getting to know anyone, I was too focused on getting out of here. I was absolutely buzzing with this new positivity, and I wanted to strike while the iron was hot.

I had a good few weeks waiting. I may have been super keen for the time to pass, but also as I had to be there, I worked on myself, on my self-esteem. I knew that to stop attracting arseholes, I would have to empower myself, to respect myself and to learn to love who I was as a person. It's not that easy after being downtrodden for so many years. Having it instilled in your psyche that you're worthless can be a hard belief to shift. Counselling helped me with that.

We didn't just talk about the relationships that I'd had. We talked about how I now felt about myself and how I could change that. I realised that I couldn't change what had happened, but I knew that I could change the way I felt about it, and the way I responded to my memories of it. I lived, and I had three fabulous children who gave me the strength to go on. I knew it was still going to be a journey to build my self-worth, but I also knew I would feel better if I could try and justify why *that man* did what he did.

While I was perusing over one of my spiritual books, I came across a story which really gleaned my interest.

A group of souls were up in heaven, choosing the purpose and goals that they would encounter in their next life. One soul stated that he needed for someone to murder him, he needed this for his soul to experience sudden death in this way, so he could grow and be closer to enlightenment. The other souls did not want to do it, they exclaimed, 'no brother, we love you, we cannot possibly kill you'. But alas, the soul said, how will I ever grow if I cannot have this experience. Still the group of souls said no, they loved him too much.

Eventually, a soul came forward and said, my brother, I love you, so much that I am willing to do this for you, I know when I kill you, you and many others will hate me, but then when we will reunite in heaven, you will understand and we will be brothers again. The original soul was overjoyed, he could go to earth and fulfil his goals to grow his soul.

Author Unknown (paraphrased)

I took so much comfort from this story. I decided that I would find peace by believing that everything that happened was to grow my soul in order to reach enlightenment. I thought it would be nicer to think of *that man* as a soul brother who helped me. Even if it turns out that there is no heaven, just devilish people, it still gave me comfort to look at it this way.

I was also learning to possess the powerful tool of forgiveness. I chose to forgive *that man* for what I had been put through. I used this tool to free myself from any ties or bonds that I had left from that relationship. I had changed in a short space of time, from being heavily depressed to being almost Buddhist like. I had gone from one extreme to the other. There was absolutely no way I could ever be in the same vicinity as *that man*, and I certainly wasn't ever going to let him have any power over me again, or any man. I deserved better.

* * *

The summer holiday finally arrived, and it was time for me to go house hunting. I went to stay at my parent's house. I was reunited with my Ellie, and life was worth living. I started phoning around every estate agent within five miles of my desired area, but they were pretty much all against social tenants.

I was becoming a little disheartened, but I couldn't give up. I only had three weeks to have Ellie back with me for good. I called and called until eventually, I got a positive response. I told the agent what I was looking for and where, and she said yes, they had what I was looking for. It had just become available and was ready for viewing the next day. The agent was even willing to pick me up from the bus stop. This was so exciting; I was viewing a house.

As the agent drove down the street, I couldn't believe my eyes. This street was beautiful, and the first thing I noticed was two huge willows directly across the road from the house. As we went in, there was a modern fitted kitchen, check, leather sofas were already in there, check, a shower and a bath, check, and a garage, check. This house was everything I had asked for from the universe. It was in my number one location too. It had excellent schools and was not too far from the city.

I was in love with it, but I didn't want to get my hopes up. I hadn't even secured funding yet for the deposit, but that was next on the agenda. I applied for a deposit and got it. I then applied for a furniture grant, and I received the highest amount. I got money for decorating, so I could move in and furnish the place how I wanted it. Thanks, Cosmos!

I couldn't wait to tell the kids, especially Ellie. She was ecstatic. I've never seen a girl so happy. I could have given her ten kittens, and she wouldn't have been this happy.

Within two weeks of finding the house, we were moving in. God, I could not wait to leave the bleak house. One year and two days we had lived there. I believe that may have been a record for a family in a women's aid refuge. If Ellie hadn't have been staying with my sister with a time limit, then I don't know how much longer we would have been there. I also did regret not looking for a house sooner. However, my new spiritual attitude was telling me that things happen for a reason. I was meant to hold out for this house. Why? Well, that's another story.

'To live is to suffer, to survive is to find some meaning in the suffering.'

~ Friedrich Nietzsche

2020

It took me a very long time to write these memoirs. I felt that I had to share my story, but it was still very difficult to convey, especially as I chose to leave it there in my past. I began writing this book in 2013. I wanted to mark the tenth anniversary of leaving the bleak house by writing about my experience there. It has taken me this long to write. So many women can't express how they feel having gone through domestic abuse. Many don't want to talk about it at all; many bottle it up for years and it eats at them. I am the opposite. I wanted my experience to be told. I thought that if my story helped just one woman to feel that she could become a survivor, then having those experiences were worth it.

When I left the bleak house, I signed up for college and began a counselling diploma. In the six years I studied, I volunteered at my local Women's Aid, and I became secretary of the group. We raised awareness about women's issues and raised funds for emergency situations. I learned to drive and got myself a little run-around car. Once my placement started in college, I held two counselling posts, one in a doctor's surgery and one in a drug and alcohol support centre. I had a bug for learning, so I then started a degree in psychology.

I threw myself into education, and I was such an immensely positive person that people around me noticed. I made a lot of friends in my neighbourhood. I may have been kidding myself a little bit, I was still definitely scarred, I was damaged goods, and learning all of the psychological theories made me very aware of that damage. It also helped me understand how experience shapes behaviour and how to change unhealthy belief systems. I was in a good place to heal myself, psychologically and spiritually.

Not long after the school term started, Nicole had made a lovely friend called Grace. They became close very quickly. I hadn't met her mum yet, but that was about to change in a very unique way. As my path of enlightenment continued, I went to bed one night, and I asked the cosmos to give me a sign about what should I be doing. I slept well, and I awoke with a word going around and around in my head, a word I'd never heard of before. 'Reiki'. Hmm? OK. I will check that out later. In the meantime, I had to get the girls ready for school.

I dropped them off, and a woman approached me, very hippie-like with swaying clothes, hair that was left to do its own thing, and a large crystal necklace.

"Hi, I'm Andrea, Grace's mum. I was wondering if Nicole would like to come for tea one night?" I told her I was happy that Nicole had made a new friend so quickly. Not much chat occurred before Andrea blurted out, "I also need to tell you that I'm a Reiki master."

My jaw hit the floor at that point, and I insisted that she wasn't, though she insisted she was. I was freaked out. She said we were meant to meet, and from there we became good friends. Andrea was like my guru, and I learned a great deal from her. I was grateful for such an insightful and positive person to be in my life. Alas, it didn't last forever, as Andrea followed her own dreams and moved to Cornwall, her spiritual home, and I was very happy for her.

Life was exciting. I had a lot going on in those first few years, and I would enjoy time with the kids and with friends. We went on our first holiday abroad, something we have continued to do. I had a car, so we went on lots of small adventures, and I had the odd night out too. I chose to remain single; I couldn't fix my damage overnight and decided it was for the best, but life was good, and I certainly wasn't lonely.

Of course, I wasn't going to get away from an abuser that easily. Eventually, he found out where I lived. I saw him driving up and down my street. I panicked, called the police, and unlike before, they listened to me. I didn't see him again after the police gave him a warning. However, I did receive a court date asking for access to the children. I never had any issues with him seeing his children, but I knew that he had no interest in them. He was just trying to regain some power over me.

I asked Nicole and Ellie if they wanted to see him and they said they would. Luke wasn't included, as his solicitor said he didn't want access to him. This was a relief to me. When the day came, my solicitor got me a private room so I wouldn't have to see him in the flesh, as all of those feelings of fear and terror came back. I had a new mindset now, but it was dangerously close to relapse just at the very thought of being anywhere near this monster. I couldn't risk my mental health again, but it was a cross I had to bear to get through this access arrangement. I told the judge he could see them. The times and dates were set, I had conditions that they were picked up at the end of the street and that if they had a party or a play through their drama club, they would be able to cancel, within reason. It was all agreed, but I knew it wouldn't last, and within a few months, he had stopped coming for them. The reason the dad of the year let them down was because he couldn't get access to me, so he dropped the kids like I knew he would. As heart-breaking as I knew it was for the children, it worked out brilliantly for me, he couldn't take me back to court, and I didn't have to send the kids to the end of the street and worry whether he would bring them back.

He didn't stop there, of course. I received a call from the girls' school asking if they had just spoken to me, I was confused, as they hadn't. So, they explained that a female coveting my identity had called to check the emergency contact details on record. The school had now given my phone number to this female. Those idiots now had my number, and boy, did they use it.

They didn't call me, not straight away, anyway. But they found more inventive ways, like taking out a handful of insurance policies in my name. I don't know what they gained from that. Yes, it was an inconvenience, but luckily, I wasn't financially out of pocket. Cancelling them was a nightmare, though. The police again were informed but couldn't do anything.

They also used my details to call the child maintenance service. I eventually plucked up the courage to apply. A payment plan was ordered; money was being taken from him, then…nothing. I called, and I asked what happened? They said I had phoned and informed them I was now being paid in cash directly. What lengths wouldn't this man go to? I calmly stated that I was aware that the calls were recorded and could they please listen to all of the calls and they would know it was two different women, which they did. The maintenance service said something about an investigation for impersonation. They told me to contact the police. Then nothing, I had no proof of anything.

Years went by from there without much of a hitch. He must have got bored. I had a strict rule not to bad-mouth that man in front of the children. I didn't want them growing up with hate and bitterness. I decided they could make up their own minds when they got older.

* * *

As time went on, I tried dating a little bit, nothing serious, just for fun. A few men came and went. Two had even met the children and my parents, but I couldn't have a relationship. I was not going to be under anyone's control. Rob fizzled out because he didn't seem to be much of a kid's guy, though he did try. Stuart had bad trust issues, and I could not be doing with that. But I did start flirting more, and I was open to some attention.

I met Nick when he came to fix my washing machine. He seemed shy, and I tried making conversation, but couldn't get much out of him. Oh well. Fast forward a year to my birthday, and my birthday night out. I was having a great night with good friends, and then I spotted my washing machine guy. I didn't realise who he was at first. I just knew he looked familiar. I approached him, and he immediately told me where I knew him from. We have been creating history ever since.

We only met up every weekend at first, and we became friends with benefits. Then he started coming around after the kids' bedtime, then sometimes at lunchtime when the kids were at school. It took a year of sneaking around before I realised that I had fallen for him. That was disastrous for me, as I didn't feel in control anymore. I didn't know what to do. All I knew was that he was a chilled, laid back guy, with a great sense of humour. He had never shown any of those tell-tale signs that he was abusive. He was supportive of everything I had plans for in my life. So, I decided to take a gamble and asked him if we should date properly. After almost five years of being single, I had a boyfriend, and it felt natural. He took his role very seriously by surprising me with a trip to New York for my birthday, and the fun, the travelling, the gestures, and the love are still going strong to this day. I found my soulmate, and we are perfect for each other. We have the same interests, our love of travel, having adventures, and sharing it all with the children. The kids adore Nick. He has been there for a big part of their lives, and we gave them a little brother too. He is there for them all and is an amazing dad. I feel blessed to have met him.

Of course, the children having a new father didn't go unnoticed. Someone reared their ugly head when Ellie put a picture of her and Nick on her Facebook profile. All of a sudden, he wanted contact again. Now able to talk to Ellie direct, he asked to see her. Ellie immediately told me what was happening, and I gave her my blessing, with one condition which was not to talk about me with him. Ellie agreed and started seeing him again, but it didn't last long. Ellie was upset that he kept bringing me up, saying I had brainwashed them into not wanting to see him, and how everything I was saying about him was wrong. Ellie was confused, as I hadn't said anything about him. I had never said they couldn't see him.

From that small era of time, Ellie came to realise that her biological father was a liar, and just wanted to get dirt on her mum. I felt sorry for her. She felt duped, but his behaviour didn't shock me, that's why I set that condition because I knew he would do that. He was very stupid to think that Ellie could be manipulated and not see what he was doing. She was a young woman with her own mind and didn't suffer fools, and this man was a fool for losing such a beautiful person from his life that was Ellie.

Eventually, Nicole suffered the same fate, and more recently, Luke did too. They have now all washed their hands of him, and it's thanks to his behaviour. They are, of course, grown-up now and can see him whenever they want, but at this point in time, they don't want to, and that's fine and dandy with me.

It's been almost seventeen years since I moved into the bleak house. They say time is a healer, and even though I am a survivor, I am not completely healed. I still have little triggers. I have noticed that I am still a control freak when it comes to my own emotions. I struggle with the idea of showing people any vulnerability, and I would rather get angry than upset. I don't want to show weakness, as I think people would start walking all over me then. It saddens me that I struggle this way, but everyone has their own coping mechanisms.

I was never -- and am still not -- strong enough to experience that hell again. I have been working hard to overcome these issues. I have a steady job, and I have been addressing all of my fears. It has taken a global pandemic for me to realise that life is too short to live in fear, and Nick and I have finally set a wedding date.

I still have a passion for all things spiritual. I became a Reiki master/teacher, a sound healing therapist, and I have trained in crystal healing, aromatherapy, hypnotherapy and past life regression, to name a few. But my big plans to grow a wellbeing service fell apart. The last four years have been pretty tough. I was diagnosed with Fibromyalgia at first, and I grieved for my life. I had been ill for years, and it took a long time to get a diagnosis. When I heard that I had a chronic illness and that I was never going to be OK again, it hit me hard. I went into a shell for a while. I was diagnosed with general anxiety disorder and depression too, and now take medication which I may need to take forever. It's a big kick in the teeth for a holistic therapist to rely on medication, but there is always room for western medicine in the holistic world.

Still, I decided not to let that diagnosis stop me. I came back fighting and decided I was going to go ahead with my big plans while I had the drive, and before I got worse. My brother, especially, was really proud of me. He wanted to see me succeed, and he was a big believer in all things holistic. Sadly, he passed away suddenly, and I had to look after my parents. The children took it hard, and I spent months in a state of utter disbelief. I still struggle to believe it. But I decided to be successful for my brother, and he would have wanted me to carry on.

I was making good progress, making connections, networking, gaining some clients, when my mum passed away suddenly. I was starting to hate life. I was barely clinging on to my hopes and dreams when the following year, my niece passed away unexpectedly. She was just one year old. I was done. I gave up life for a good six months. I became withdrawn, down, and the signs of depression were showing. I was still struggling to come to terms with my brother passing. My mum and niece had to join a queue. I'm still waiting to process them, and my fear is that I will lose the plot with all of the pain that I am putting off. Every cloud, however, does have a silver lining, and while I took time out of life, I finally wrote this book.

This is where I am now. I have a great life. I'm still living in the same street, I have three grown-up children and Harry, who are all amazing. Ellie has a good job and lives with her boyfriend. Nicole is in university, Luke is in college, and Harry is in school. They are all well-balanced, kind young people, and I couldn't be prouder of them. Luke more than anyone, as he was diagnosed with a congenital heart condition when he was twelve, Wolfe Parkinson White Syndrome. He has had two procedures to date and will need more, and he is very brave. He took me to one side when he was seventeen and told me that he was OK with death. He didn't want me to worry and if it was his time, then so be it. I cried. The kids had seen a lot of death in a short space of time, and with Luke regularly being rushed into hospital with a racing heart rate, he has a lot of hospital walls. This is something we live with every day, and with so many people I love dying suddenly, I am struggling with Luke's condition.

Although Luke and I have our health issues, and I have a heavy heart, I still appreciate how good my life is. I have a naturally positive nature, so I will always bounce back up no matter what life throws at me. I decided to not continue with my holistic therapy venture and to get a regular job working in care. I couldn't be happier with my job. Caring for people is what I do best.

* * *

My aim, when writing this book, wasn't to highlight the abuse I suffered, but to give hope to other women. By telling my story, I want women to know that they can be free from abuse and that they can have a life without being controlled. My message is simple, though I know the implications of trying to get free can be very difficult. It can happen. You can do it.

Going through a refuge was very hard. This book is not about tarnishing the work that Women's Aid does. Without the refuge, I don't know where I would be today. They helped me, and I am very grateful, but it was tough going. I want people to know that as hard as it was, I came out the other side, stronger than ever. Women's Aid are saving women's lives, and if you feel unsafe, please contact them.

HELPLINE NUMBERS:

Women's Aid Domestic Abuse Helpline 0808 2000 247

The Men's Advice Line 0808 801 0327

The Mix (under 25's) 0808 808 4994

National LGBT and Domestic Abuse Helpline 0800 999 5428

National Stalking Helpline 0808 802 0300

ACKNOWLEDGEMENTS

I would like to say a big thank you to everyone who has encouraged me to write this story. I couldn't have done this without a lot of little voices chipping away. One of those is the lovely Sue Miller from Team Author UK, without whom this book would not be out there at all. It's taken a while, but we got there in the end.

ABOUT THE AUTHOR

Lal Kelly is an ordinary British woman from North Wales who has had some extraordinary life experiences. Lal lives in the north-west of England with her family and two dogs,
Missy and Marni.

Much of Lal's life has been filled with torment and tragedy, and yet this is a lady who has overcome it all and enjoys a life full of laughter, love and positive experiences.

Lal loves music events, and she is a radio producer and host for a local radio station.

Lal loves to travel and experience culture and history from around the globe. Her favourite place is Venice.

In 2017, Lal won the Bizmums Inspirational Mum award for overcoming hurdles in life and using those experiences to help others.

For more information, please visit:

www.lalkelly.com

Please follow on Social Media:

www.facebook.com/LalKellyUK

www.twitter.com/lalKelly1

www.instagram.com/lal.kelly

Printed in Great Britain
by Amazon

52328444R00140